This book is dedicated to all the brothers and sisters
of Sylvia Epstein Press

Frontispiece: *The Rock Drill* (Jacob Epstein, 1913-14), bronze (cast 1962) 28″ x 26″ on wood base 12″ diameter. Collection, The Museum of Modern Art, New York. Mrs. Simon Guggenheim.

THE EPSTEINS
A FAMILY ALBUM
by Jane F. Babson

TAYLOR HALL PUBLISHING

Published in the United Kingdom by Taylor Hall Publishing Ltd,
P O Box 156, Chearsley, Aylesbury

© Jane F Babson *1984*

ISBN 0 907807 01 1

Typeset by Proset. Artwork by Profile Art Services (London)
Printed by Molesey Litho (Surrey)

ACKNOWLEDGMENTS

The author wishes to recognize the efforts of many who have aided in providing data on the subjects covered in this book. Through their help and cooperation, either by their assistance or knowledge, I have been able to put together both the records on the tapes and this study and story. Some helped with the historical assessment of the culture on the Lower East Side of New York City, either through help with the Epstein house on Hester Street, or with background material. Others helped me with my studies of the family and its members, the costumes and fashion industry, the garment district, the early movie industry, and the art and life of Sir Jacob Epstein. I am very grateful to all the following people:

The Office of the former Vice President of the United States, Walter F. Mondale, and Senator Jacob K. Javits, for their assistance in calling attention to the house at 102 Hester Street to the National Register of Historic Places; the late Dr. Irving Epstein for his memories; the late Abner Dean for his insights into the family; the late Miss Florence Solomon for her personal family photographs; Mrs. Leatrice Joy Gilbert and Miss Blanche Sweet for their data on movies and New York in the 1900s; Miss Lillian Gish for her courtesy in examining our photograph of Al Press, Mrs. Eileen Bowser, Former Curator of Film, Museum of Modern Art, New York, for her research into the career of Alexander Press; also Mr. Samuel A. Gill, Curator of the Academy of Motion Picture Arts and Sciences, Hollywood; Mr. Julian Plowden, Paramount Pictures, and Mrs. Rose Weinberg, former secretary to the late Adolph Zukor, for their help in my search for Mr. Press's movie career; Mr. C.S. Dickson, Cunard, New York, and Mr. D.J. Biggs, Cunard, Southampton, England, for help in finding information on ocean voyages; Mr. J.T. O'Neill, the University of Liverpool, England, for his information on pleasure cruises and Aquitania *Cruise to Nowhere*; Mr. Richard J. Koke, Curator of the Museum, The New York Historical Society, Ms. Esther Brumberg, Photoarchivist, Museum of the City of New York, Ms. Rhonda Kahn, The Jewish Museum, New York City, for aid in my search for pictorial representations of Hyam Salomon and help with photographs of Hester Street; the Consulate General of the Polish People's Republic, New York, for research into the family records in Augustów, Poland; the late Mr. Robert Rickles, and his wife, Merle Rickles, Mrs. Beverly Spatt and Mr. Kent L. Barwick, New York Landmarks Commission, for their attention to the Epstein house; Mrs. Claudia Kidwell, Associate Curator, the National Museum of American History, Smithsonian Institution, Washington, D.C., for her help with costumes; Mr. John Rose, Public Information, the Metropolitan Museum of Art, New York, and Mr. Lowery B. Sims, Assistant Curator, The Metropolitan Museum, for his pictures of Epstein's *Relief, The Sun God*; Ms. Dian Spitler, Senior Librarian, Atlantic City Free Public Library, Atlantic City, New Jersey, for help in providing me with early magazines of the resort; members of the staff of the New York Public Library, in particular the special divisions devoted to the arts, and the Jewish Division, for help with Yiddish; also the staffs of the Greenwich Library, Greenwich, Connecticut, and the Ferguson Library, Stamford, Connecticut. Nicholas Philippas, Keith Barrett, Hildreth Kupik, and George Kontaxis are to be thanked for their attention to my photographs, both the development of mine and the Epstein family photographs used in this book. Mr. David Ogunleye, Security, Riverside Church, New York City, deserves special recognition for his aid to me which enabled me to photograph the Riverside Church's *Madonna and Child*.

In England, a special acknowledgment is due The Very Reverend Alun H. Davies, M.A., Dean of Llandaff Cathedral, Llandaff, Wales, and Mr. Neville James, also of Llandaff; the personnel of Lewis's Department Store, Liverpool; the staff of Hyde Park for their assistance in my photography of *Rima The Hudson Memorial*; Mr. George Breeze, Assistant Keeper, City Art Museum, Birmingham, for making it possible for the *Lucifer* to be photographed; and the personnel at the Café Royal, London, who verified the story of Epstein and the wine bottle and provided insight into the Café's clientele. I reserve a special thanks to my British solicitor, D.H. Benham, Esq., for his advice and efforts toward publication, and to Karen Pilkington, his assistant.

In Paris the assistance of le Conservateur and the personnel of Père Lachaise Cemetery is gratefully acknowledged.

I am also very grateful for the assistance of my husband, David F. Babson, Jr., for legal advice, Mr. Ronald J. St. Onge, my copyright attorney, Stamford, and my Washington attorneys, Mr. Bruce J. Terris and Mr. James Hecker, for their work toward naming the school now being erected on the site of the Epstein house for Sir Jacob Epstein, and to Mrs. Sonia Maguire and the late Miss Sylvie Blein, friends, and in the latter case, former wardrobe mistress to the late Geraldine Farrar, Stamford. Their memories of the career and life of the great diva added valuable background material. Mrs. Lilly Stunzi, Rowayton, Connecticut, is also to be thanked for her memories of Lillian Wald, the Henry Street Settlement, and Mrs. Stunzi's memories of her experience as one of the proprietors of a cooperative grocery store established on Henry Street, New York, for indigent Jewish families.

Bibliographical Acknowledgements

It was decided that the nature of the material for this book did not lend itself to a detailed bibliography and such an addition might mislead the reader as to the real sources for this book. Most of the material was gained from primary sources and in great part from the people who were related to, or knew, Sir Jacob Epstein, or those who were actively involved during this period of our history. However, there are several acknowledgments which are essential to the understanding of how the book was written, and they are as follows:

The material concerning the ideas and designs used by Mrs. Press in her designs for her dress company were taken from our interview recorded on tape when Jane Babson, Marthe Clamage, and Mrs. Press were viewing the exhibition, *American Women of Style,* which ran from December 13, 1975 to August 31, 1976, at The Metropolitan Museum of Art. This exhibition was organized by Mrs. Diana Vreeland, Special Consultant to the Costume Institute, Metropolitan Museum of Art. We were further helped in getting our material on this subject by the exhibition, *Suiting Everyone,* and the catalog by the same name, The National Museum of History and Technology, Smithsonian Institution, Washington, D.C. This permanent exhibition of American Ready-to-Wear was partly responsible for the ideas which became this book.

A great deal of the material used in this book came from information supplied by the American family members of Sir Jacob Epstein. Sir Jacob Epstein's two autobiographical works, Epstein, Jacob, *Let There Be Sculpture,* G. P. Putnam's Sons, New York (copyright 1940 Jacob Epstein) (revised and republished as Epstein, Sir Jacob, *Epstein, An Autobiography,* E.P. Dutton and Company, Inc., New York, 1955) and Epstein, Jacob to Arnold Haskell, *The Sculptor Speaks,* William Heinemann Ltd, London, 1931, contained many clues as to the understanding of his monumental works. The information concerning Margaret Epstein, Epstein's first wife, was obtained from Mrs. Press and from personal letters from Mrs. Margaret Epstein to Mrs. Press. A great deal of valuable insight was also gained from personal correspondence from Epstein and his daughter Peggy Jean to Mrs. Press. This aided in understanding the artist as a son, husband, and father. Personal photographs, taken of the early Epstein sculpture made around 1902 at the École des Beaux Arts (art which was destroyed by the other students) showed me Epstein's abilities while he was a young student in Paris. These photographs were owned by the late Abner Dean.

It was necessary to read from a great number of sources to provide adequate knowledge of this period. Besides books on fashion designers, Art Déco, and the Follies, etc., Hutchins Hapgood's *The Spirit of the Ghetto,* Schocken Books, New York, 1966, with annotations by Harry Golden, was used extensively while studying the family background. Harry Golden's own books on the Jewish family and the Lower East Side of New York helped greatly in developing background. The autobiographies of Eddie Cantor, Anita Loos, Lillian Gish, and Marion Davies were also valuable. Gertrude Stein's *The Autobiography of Alice Toklas* and *Wars I Have Seen* were used and Ronald Sanders, *The Downtown Jews,* Signet Edition, New York, 1977, was most helpful, as was Leo Rosten's *The Joys of Yiddish,* McGraw-Hill Book Company, New York, 1968. The study of Yiddish stories, jokes and the meaning of Yiddish words provided a major understanding of events in the lives of both Mrs. Press and Sir Jacob Epstein. The life and poetry of Oscar Wilde were read and studied, as was John Milton's *Paradise Lost,* parts of Dante's *Inferno* and the poetry of Walt Whitman. A major study was made of W.H. Hudson's *Green Mansions,* and The Holy Bible. Another important book which provided new information was B.L. Reid's *The Man from New York, John Quinn and his Friends,* Oxford University Press, New York, 1968. The only art reference book used which concerned itself with Epstein's art was Richard Buckle, *Jacob Epstein, Sculptor,* Faber and Faber, Ltd., London, 1963; it provided valuable chronology and insight into Epstein's *oeuvre.*

Real insight into Epstein's monumental work was gained by listening to the British Broadcasting Corporation's taped interview by Wyn Roberts in April 1957 with Sir Jacob Epstein at Llandaff Cathedral, while both were viewing the *Majestas* (Ref. No. YLO 64713). In this interview Epstein remarks that the sculpture is very suited to the environment and that it is a direct development from the early work *The Visitation,* a work of simplicity and serenity. Epstein remarks that out of *The Visitation* came the *Madonna and Child* of Cavendish Square, and out of that work was derived *Majestas.* Epstein regarded the *Majestas* to be one of his best works to date.

In an attempt to understand the Epstein family life early photographs of Hester Street and the Lower East Side were studied in the collections of The New York Public Library, The Museum of the City of New York, and The New York Historical Society. Early engravings of New York at the turn of the century were also studied. In-depth studies were made in the Egyptian *Book of the Dead,* in particular the Hieroglyphic Transcript of the Papyrus of Ani, the translation into English and an introduction by E.A. Wallis Budge, Late Keeper of the Egyptian and Assyrian Antiquities in the British Museum, Bell Publishing Company, New York, (republication of the 1900 London edition) and *The Kabbalah, The Religious Philosophy of the Hebrews,* translated by Adolphe Franck, first edition, 1843, and retranslated from I Sossnitz, New York, 1926, by Bell Publishing Company, New York, 1960.

Epstein's art was studied both in America and in Europe. The Middle East provided me with a major insight when I visited Palmyra, Syria, and The National Museum in Damascus. In Damascus I saw the original Jewish frescoes from the synagogue at Dura Europos.

After this manuscript was completed, *Smile, Please, An Unfinished Biography*, by Jean Rhys, Harper & Row,1979, was published. I have long been an admirer of Miss Rhys and have read all of her work. Her *Quartet*, 1928, has particularly intrigued and fascinated me. I have also read Ford Madox Ford's writing and have never believed that the "German" couple, the Heidlers, in *Quartet* were Ford Madox Ford and his wife, or *amour*. When I read *Smile, Please*, I was struck by the similarity of Mrs. Press's and Miss Rhys' faces in old age. I compared Mrs. Press's picture at the end of this book with Miss Rhys' (see back cover of her autobiography) – the large eyes, the blond hair are very close.

Further study of *Quartet* led me to the conclusion that the Heidlers are Jacob and Margaret Epstein, artistically reversed in some respects, especially age. Heidler is described by Miss Rhys as having a breakdown in World War I, as being quite tall, and having strange eyes. At the end of *Quartet* there is a description of Heidler as a cold "God". I think that Epstein and Miss Rhys were lovers, and their relationship, with Margaret, is artfully described in this book. I think that Miss Rhys' description of Epstein as "God", Heidler, may be, in part, the seed for the later *"Majestas"*, Cardiff.

There are many obscure references to the "German" couple in Miss Rhys's stories. The woman is described as keeping cats. Although I do not believe that Miss Rhys was her mother, I think that Epstein's first daughter, Peggy Jean, was named after Margaret Epstein and Jean Rhys. Jean Rhys may have been Epstein's first serious love after his first marriage. Miss Rhys was an actress who frequented the Crabtree, a known haunt of Epstein's. She mentions in her autobiography that Epstein did a portrait of Lilliane Shelley. In Buckle's, *Jacob Epstein, Sculptor*, page 100, plate 159, there is a bronze portrait called *Head of a Girl*, done 1916-1920 period. A comparison of the features of this work with Jean Rhys' family photographs in her book, which show her as a young woman, indicate that this is her portrait.

Miss Rhys' description of the pain of this relationship is moving, but Epstein's pain is only hinted at and never explored, nor is Margaret's. It is mitigated in part by the great art which it produced.

rs, where known,
ly acknowledged.

·25, 33 & 36.

ɔn, Washington

Plate 31: by Permission of the Dean and Chapter of Llandaff Cathedral, Cardiff, Wales, (photographer: S Travers AIBP)
Plate 36: courtesy of Manchester City Art Galleries, England and London Art Service Ltd
Plates 59 & 60: courtesy of the Metropolitan Museum of Art, New York

LIST OF PLATES

PROLOGUE

We were friends, Sylvia Press, Marthe Clamage and I. We enjoyed one another's company and in our visits together I would listen to their stories about their famous brother and uncle, Sir Jacob Epstein. "You should write a book," I would say, and they would laugh and say no. On Christmas Day 1975 they came to visit me and asked me to write their story. During the years that followed, we began taping their memories. This culminated in an artistic breakthrough which I can now only explain as a pyschic experience.

It slowly became apparent to me that there was more to this story than I had been able to find in our interviews. I began to study the family, and historical New York City, (for Sir Jacob Epstein had mentioned in his writings how important this was to him). At the same time I was transcribing the tapes and studying the interviews as they progressed.

On April 18 1977 I went to Davis and Long Gallery in New York City to see their exhibition on British Vorticism. I concentrated my attention on Epstein's works there, in particular his drawings of the period from 1909 to 1915 and the sculpture. I was struck by the two pieces, *The Sunflower*, 1910, and *The Rock Drill*, 1913-1915. As I stood looking at the *Rock Drill* I began to see the separate components of the work and I saw that the key to Epstein's monumental works was before me. I knew that there was an extraordinary story to tell.

When I started to write the book it was necessary to formulate a style based on several elements and to go back into time, to Sylvia and Jacob Epstein's youth. What was the age in which they lived?

This was a time which unfortunately has almost disappeared from our society. It was a period of immense vitality, when great artists were our idols and the developing garment industry and movies offered opportunities for the Jewish children of the Lower East Side of New York City. They would out of necessity develop their abilities and establish themselves in the evolving American society. Their extraordinary contributions to art, science, literature, music, social reform, entertainment, and to businesses such as fashion, the garment industry, and movies influenced the culture and history of the world.

This was a time when the beautiful Ziegfeld Girl, dressed in her dazzling gowns, furs and jewels, represented a goddess-like attainment for women. Her operatic counterpart, Geraldine Farrar, sang regularly with her co-star, Enrico Caruso, for the Kaiser and Kaiserin's birthday celebrations. This beautiful woman with her extraordinary voice was courted by the Crown Prince of Germany. Lou Tellegen, the model for Rodin's *Eternal Spring* and one of Sarah Bernhardt's last leading men, was married to Farrar for a time. "Gerry Flappers" crowded the opera star's path and sent her so many flowers that she stood knee-deep in them on stage. Lillian Gish and Blanche Sweet were the early "sweetheart" stars of the movies. At the same time Helena Rubinstein, Hannah Troy and Sylvia Epstein were employed in American industries as both owner-designers and workers. All of these women maintained a precarious balance, juggling equally the images of little girl, siren, sweetheart, mother and career-woman. They did it intuitively and only dimly recognized that is was necessary. This was strange and uniquely American, an amalgam of the sophistication and naïveté contributed to American society by a flourishing immigrant population. We are still working out the problems which it has presented to us. Within this balance so shakily maintained it is possible that there lie solutions to the dilemmas of present-day women. This past age is our age too; it is all one time and we are only now beginning to see this. Sylvia Press's life is only one solution to the problem of women, and to the problem of being a member of a family where one child is a world-famous celebrity. Perhaps her solutions point up ours, for each solution must be individual and personal fulfillment cannot be relegated to others.

It should be noted here that when Mrs. Press was first interviewed for this book she was eighty years old. The interviews continued for two years. Mrs. Press had written a short manuscript when she was attending The New School for Social Research in New York City in the early 1940s. She also kept a short diary during her visit to the Epsteins in London in 1928. I have combined the diary, the manuscript and the material on the tapes, and the greater part of the book is written in a style composed of many of her own words. Her tapes provided an extraordinary recall of her brother, Sir Jacob Epstein, the other family members, their careers and families, and life on the Lower East Side of New York City as well as Upper Manhattan. There is also an account of her career in the garment industry at the time of its greatest development. She dressed us in fashions by Paul Poiret – "all for $29.95".

While working on the project we found the Epstein house on Hester Street and it was proposed by me, along with Hester Street, to the United States National Register of Historic Places. Despite all my efforts, officials in New York ignored the fact that the house was before the Register for listing and they destroyed it in April, 1980. An intermediate school is being erected on the site. Legal efforts are now underway to name this school after Sir Jacob Epstein and to place a proper commemorative plaque on the site. The United States has yet to understand that our artists contribute something to our society which may be greater than our business and scientific accomplishments. Their art is an eternal monument to times and people now gone forever.

If there are errors in this book they are not deliberate ones nor are they misrepresentations of truth. Mrs. Sylvia Epstein Press died on December 11, 1980, at the end of the Chanukah celebration. I attended her funeral on the day that mass memorial services were held in New York City and throughout the world for the Liverpool giant of rock music, John Lennon.

My friend, Marthe Epstein Clamage, died on January 29, 1983. A number of other friends who helped with this book have also died, but art, literature, music and the human spirit will not die. They are immortal.

Jane F. Babson

CONTENTS

CHAPTER ONE

My father ruled the roost. He was a short, pompous man, but rather good looking, and as far back as I can recollect, my father was king of our household. When I was very small we lived on New York City's Lower East Side at 102 Hester Street. 102 Hester is still there. I saw it again in 1976 for the first time since I was little. It is *still* there, with two front windows for shops and a high metal stoop. There are apartments (we called them flats) in the five-storey, red brick tenement, just as there used to be, but one side of the shops is Frankie's Coffeeshop. My father had a bakery on one side of the shop door and a grocery store on the other. We had a six-room apartment on the first floor, three rooms each, divided by a stairway which ran down the center.

We were very comfortable people for the neighborhood. My father invested in real estate and built buildings on the Lower East Side, first with his son-in-law, Jacob Stone, and later with my oldest brother. He also built buildings in Harlem with his niece's husband, who was a Cohn. This man Cohn's son owned The American Book Company, wholesale booksellers. There used to be a big sign on one of the buildings up in Harlem, Park Avenue and 112th Street, *Epstein and Cohn*. I think if the building is still there, it's still *Epstein and Cohn*.

My father loved America. That was the golden land to him. He was born in Augustów, Poland, in 1859, the same town that Senator Edmund Muskie's father came from. In 1859 it was Russian Poland and they sent him to America when he was eleven because when he got to be thirteen he had to join the army. He was the youngest in the family. Alone they sent him. His older brother was already in America some years. My father came in 1870 on a half a ticket, while his mother stayed in Poland. She joined him later, but my father's father had died some time before he left and his mother, whose first name was Lena, remarried. I don't know my father's father's first name but the family name was not Epstein. It was Barntovsky and my father's Jewish name was Chatskel, Chatskel Barntovsky. Later, in America, he took the name Max for his common name.

He went first to Whitechapel, London, England, and then to America, where his brother had remarried and changed his name to Epstein, a name belonging to the brother's wife in America. When Chatskel got to Castle Garden in New York he was left on the boat; he was the only one, speaking no English. They couldn't find him and then they said to his brother; "Well, this must be your little brother."

"Yes, that's my little brother."

"Well, he's got a different name on the tag, " said the immigration officials.

"I took my wife's name, " said his brother and so the inspectors said:

"Well, if your name is Epstein, his name is Epstein." And that's how he got the name Epstein. While we were writing this book we wrote to Augustów for the birth records or any other kind, but records of this type in Augustów now start only from 1946, so you will have to take my word for family origins.

I don't know where he lived in New York. I know he went to work in a shop, a sewing shop, you know – tailoring. He was a tailor's assistant and he never knew anything about that. He didn't like it. He didn't like it. He immediately stopped it. He said he grew up when he was seventeen years old, for he wanted to marry the man's daughter, the man who used to give out the bread and *matzohs* in his town, Augustów. My mother's father and mother were millers of the town and they used to, every Friday, make bread, rolls and things like that to give to the poor people and they used to stand in line. He remembers he was sent to pick up the bread. He said he must marry that man's daughter.

My mother, Mary Solomon, was in America a few years before, with her parents, Isaac and Boschye (Sarah) Solomon. They came while Lincoln was president, in 1865. I don't remember them, my grandparents; they died before I was born, a few months or a year, I think. They're buried in Washington Cemetery in Brooklyn. All my family such as mother and father and some of the relatives were buried there by the Tel Torah d'Augustów Society. This society was formed by the people from the same town in Poland. When my mother came over she was about six, I think, and her two sisters were two and four years old. My mother always claimed that one of her uncles, possibly a great uncle, was Haym Salomon, who financed the American Revolution. He was from Poland and Solomon can be spelled both ways. According to my father, his uncle was Barney Barnato of the Kimberly Mines in Africa, and when the old man died my father put in a claim to his estate, but he said there were too many children and he didn't get anything.

My mother's people were all very comfortable and her brothers were brought up not to work. I don't know what my father's father did. I heard that he painted a fresco on the temple wall in Augustów. My father said that he remembered that people came from all the different towns to see it. He told me that his father died right after that. My father also said that my grandfather was thirty-four years old when he died. I think after that my grandmother Lena remarried; who, I don't know.

After he got here my father had to learn English, so he had a private teacher to come in to teach him. He couldn't go to school because he had to work. My mother also had very little schooling here and I don't think that there was anyone on my mother's side who had artistic talent. My mother was a pretty, tall, plump girl with lovely red hair, and as I said, my father was very good looking. They were married when they were both seventeen, my mother being six months older than my father. Neither of my parents was particularly Semitic-looking and my mother looked like a handsome Irish woman. I remember at 102 Hester Street a lot of mother's tenants were Irish, and one, a Mrs. Anderson, used to say to her: "Mrs. Epstein, Mary, *how* could you marry a little Jew like that"?

My mother used to say to her: "But Mrs. Anderson, I'm a Jewess."

"Oh, no," she would say. "You're not a Jewess. You're a typical Irishwoman." She wouldn't believe my mother was Jewish. Almost all the people down on Hester and the other streets were either Jewish, Irish or Italian. Now it's black, Porto Rican, Chinese, some Italian; how it has changed with different people, but the street looks pretty much the same. My parents rented out our upstairs to the different families. My mother and father used to say that there was one girl who lived in one of our rooms, a showgirl, who later married an English lord. "My God!" they used to say. "She married a *lord*."

I can't remember her name. I think her first name was Mae. Mother also said that Eddie Cantor lived in one of their rooms at 102 Hester when he was very small, about two or three years old; he lived there with his grandmother Esther, who brought him up. We haven't been able to prove this. My father put a bathroom in on the first floor, in our apartment. That was very unusual and my mother, who was very kind, used to let her tenants come downstairs to take a bath sometimes. My father used to bawl her out. She was giving everything away, he said. The toilets were in the rear of the house, in the yard, so you can see what a luxury a bath was. It was the only flat in the building with a bath.

My mother helped my father in the store and bakery. I have a slight recollection of it because I was around four when we moved uptown. They supplied the surrounding groceries with bread and rolls and today would be called a bakery supplier with a route. My mother was usually pregnant but she always worked in the store. She was very kind to people who came in. If they didn't have anything, she would fill their baskets up with all kinds of things. I remember she would give them food. She was very good-natured.

We employed two Polish maids to clean the six rooms in our flat. They helped my mother with the washing and cooking and they helped with the hard work in the building, in place of a janitor. They did not take care of our large family, the size of which was typical of the time. My mother had twelve children, twelve, and eight lived. That's enough, what with the work of helping and always being pregnant, like all the other women of those days.

The first one of my parents' children was my brother Louis, who was born soon after my parents married. I think Lou was born around 1877. My sister Ida was born next, around 1878 or 1879, and my brother Jacob was born November 10, 1880. Hyman was born August 28, 1882 and then my sister Chana came on December 1, 1884. We called her Honey, or Annie – she was so sweet and kind. She always signed her name Annie Epstein. My mother had a child or two who died before my brother Irving was born in 1891, and there was a child born between Irving and me; it died. I was born Susie Epstein on March 23, 1895. I was supposed to be the last but after me came my little brother Harold, who was born on December 4, 1899. Jacob and all the rest of us were born at 102 Hester Street. We had a doctor, Dr. Berlinger, to attend my mother and deliver us, which was unusual for those days.

Harold and I were the babies to the rest of the children. I remember when Harold was born. I was four years old. My mother had just had Harold. I ran out onto the stoop at 102 Hester. "My mother had a baby! My mother had a baby!" My brother Louey and my sister Ida were there and they pulled me in and started to hit me. My father said: "Did you people go crazy? She's very happy that her mother had a baby. Why are you carrying on like that?"

There used to be pushcarts up and down the street. Hester Street was full of pushcarts, clothes, fruit, food, everything, everything. The men used to say to my parents: "Your little girl took a banana." Or: "Your little girl took a pear." And my parents would pay. I don't know whether I took the things or not; I suppose I did. Around the corner on Eldridge was the firm of men's clothing called Witty Brothers. That company is still down there. They're wholesalers now. My brother-in-law Jacob Stone's sister Jenny's husband Sam ran that company. He and his brother Henry made fine men's suits and my father used to buy his suits there. He'd pay one hundred, one hundred and ten dollars a suit, and he used to order two or three at a time. My father had money.

I remember once I was playing on Chrystie Street with my two little cousins, two young girls, and they were barefoot. So I took off my shoes and my father came along. He got very angry when he saw me and he said to me: "Put your shoes back on. We're not like that. You wear your shoes."

A year or so ago I was down on Houston Street on a Sunday to look around. A policeman came up to me and said: "Lady, don't ever come down here on a Sunday."

I said: "Why?"

He said: "It's impossible." And then he said: "Lady, have you never been down here?"

I really laughed inside. I wanted to tell him: "I was born down here."

CHAPTER TWO

We were considered an attractive family and all the children had blue eyes, most being fair-haired. It's funny but the children who were dark did look Irish with their blue eyes. Another funny thing is that we children all had what we call the Epstein face. It was really Mary Epstein's face with a little variation. The same nose, lips, eyes, everything. All of us were tall like my mother's family, except Honey, who was short like my father. She was pretty and plump as it was the fashion to be buxom in those days. My sister Ida was dark-haired and tall. The baby, Harold, was called Pee Wee because he was little. Of course, he and I were very small when Jacob was growing up. We heard stories about him from the other family members. Jacob had been sick for a long time when he was very small and had to be carried around. I don't know what illness he had; maybe it was a lung ailment.

Anyway, Jacob was a dreamy sort of child and sometimes was a problem. During the Great Blizzard of 1888, my father was supplying the poor people in the house with food from his bakery and grocery. They got it through the back door of his store in the building. The snow had completely blocked the front, piling up to the second storey, and no one could get outside. My father missed quite an amount of bagels, rolls and bread and he searched all over for it. Finally they found it. Jacob had hidden all the bread and rolls. My sister Ida told me that Jacob spoke up and said: "I'll have enough to eat."

Jacob was a real mystery to Max Epstein, who used to say he didn't understand how he had come to such a *meshuggener* son. "If you want to be a lawyer, if you want to be a doctor – but an artist? You'll starve." my father said to him. Jacob was always reading or drawing, drawing all day. He'd draw the women on the stoop nursing their babies, or the old Jewish men with their long beards. Anything that my father considered ugly, Jacob would draw.

At P.S. Seven on Chrystie Street, where the older Epstein children went to school, Jacob would always be excused from subjects so that he could draw anything that came to mind. On the blackboard he'd do Christmas, Easter, Spring and Autumn. He was also forever reading under a green-shaded lamp at home. The house could burn down under him; he was that oblivious. I remember how Jacob looked then. Of course, I was a youngster and my memories are slight, but he was tall and slender. He was very good-looking, very handsome. He had beautiful deep-set eyes, the same color blue we all had, a deep, greyish blue. He had very black, curly hair and he had a beautiful build. He was very virile, very masculine. All the Epstein boys were tall, with good builds, and very virile.

I have memories of when Jacob used to set me on the kitchen table at 102 Hester Street and paint or draw me. I had on, one time, a bright red flannel petticoat. My mother had made it on the sewing machine. It was sleeveless, with a full skirt and a cut-out neck. Jacob was painting me. I was about three years old then. I was a very thin child and I had long blond hair with blue eyes. That's all I remember of it. I remember also that Jacob used to carry me around on his shoulders. I never went with him on his walks around Hester Street. I was too little. Honey went with him. She was a great friend of his; they were near in age and Honey understood him better than anyone else, better than my mother and certainly better than my father. After he died, Jacob's second wife, Lady Kathleen, wrote me that he always told her how he remembered me, his little sister with the long, golden hair.

Most of the Epstein children were obedient and my father had no trouble making them behave. Max Epstein was very selfish. He thought he had a family for his own convenience and they should do and say for him, to help make things easier for him. He had no understanding of a boy like Jacob. My mother always tried to make excuses for him and to smooth things over. She always said that Jacob would be a great man; my father said he would starve. I remember when I went down to see *Social Consciousness* a few years ago in Philadelphia. I started to cry, and I said to my niece Marthe: "Mother never knew how great he was." She didn't but she recognized his special qualities. My father was indifferent to all his children's ambitions.

My mother was a very simple woman. She was all for her husband, her family, and the house. She wanted all her children to go to college. My father didn't care as much as my mother. She took great pride in having her children educated. The girls didn't have to go to school then, but the boys did. They were sent to school and the boys all received religious education. My father had a rabbi come every day, every day, to teach them. He came to the house. I received no religious training at all. My father didn't believe in it for girls.

After P.S. Seven, Jacob went to the East Side Settlement School, then he won a contest at Cooper Union and went there and to the Art Students League. He also taught at the Educational Alliance, where he knew Rose Pastor, the Russian Jewish girl who married the millionaire, Graham Stokes. That was the talk of the Hester Street area then; it was a mixed marriage. Another person he knew was the anarchist, Emma Goldman. Jacob was an anarchist too, in his early days. I remember a priceless story about Emma Goldman.

She came to the house on Hester Street on a Passover to get Jacob to go to some kind of anarchist meeting. My father was furious. *"Deh bummerkeh,"* he said, *"raus a mein haus."* It means: "You tramp," in Yiddish, "get out of my house." He wouldn't let Jacob go. He objected to everything about her; my father was very patriotic. Jacob said that he was willing to speak for her, but not on a Passover. Of course the anarchists on the Lower East Side weren't the kind you had in Europe, crazy and violent. They were idealistic, but my father did not approve of that kind of politics.

While Jacob was attending the Settlement he met people of another social stratum, people who had come down there to work for social betterment. One of the people who took a special interest in him and his work was Mrs. Stuyvesant Fish. She took quite a fancy to him and sent a letter to my dad, explaining that she had lost her son in the Spanish American War. She said she could be of value to Jacob and could further his art, for she could give him the advantages she knew his father could not. She asked if she could adopt him as her son. Now my dad was far from poor and this enraged him. He was furious at Jacob for inviting such a request. Jacob didn't know of the letter, of course, until it was received. Mrs. Stuyvesant Fish used to send an open barouche for him. Do you know what that is? It was a carriage with two horses, a footman and a driver. They would call for Jacob and take him and his oil paintings up to her house, where she gave teas. She would buy his paintings and sometimes sell some for him. Finally Jacob got tired of that and he told his mother that he was not going up there any more, not to that rich woman's house. He did make some money this way. Jacob would give some of the money he earned to his mother, but she would always return it when no one was around. With this money he was able to rent a studio in an old rickety house in Greenwich Village.

At one time my father owned forty-two tenements on the Lower East Side. He would buy houses from the government for very little money; they needed money, and he would buy them and then sell them as he needed money. Around 1902 my father sold some of his old tenements which had been condemned by the city. They made Seward Park on the site; it was a playground for ghetto children. Because of his athletic build and abilities, Jacob was made a physical education instructor. After two weeks in the park, Jacob came home and told his mother that a friend of his, also a young, struggling artist, Bernard Gussow, was up against it and had no money to live on. Jacob insisted that the department install Gussow as the physical education instructor. Jacob got himself another job as an inspector with the Tenement House Department. He then reported his father and his uncle because they had violations on their buildings' fire escapes. They let people sleep on the fire escapes, with bedding there and all. My father and uncle came down and they said to Jacob: "What's the matter? What's wrong?"

Jacob said to them: "Well, first you have to start with your own home. Your own place."

About this time Jacob went off with Gussow to live in the woods during the winter. They went to Greenwood, New Jersey, and there they sketched, hunted and fished for their food.

Then there was the time a fire destroyed all his paintings in the old building where he had the garret studio. Jacob worked some in our house at 102 Hester Street, made sketches there, but he had rooms down there which were his studios. After the fire he had to start all over again. We had moved away by that time, up to 1661 Madison Avenue. Jacob didn't like the move. He kept a room there with us, but he never worked there, and spent little time in the house. He would come up sometimes to see my mother. This was the last place he lived with us in America, and he spent most of his time on the Lower East Side after we had moved away. He would go to the courts and sketch heads of the different criminals who were being tried, and then sell the sketches to the newspapers. Of course most people know about his first real commission, Hutchins Hapgood's *The Spirit of the Ghetto*. With the money he earned as illustrator of that book, and the sales of a few oils sold in a society woman's salon, he paid his passage to Europe. He was nineteen when we moved uptown; I was four and Harold was an infant. My father gave up his grocery business and devoted himself to building and managing his real estate with his son, niece's husband and son-in-law.

Max Epstein constantly ridiculed Jacob's ambitions and was ashamed of his son's talents. Jacob wanted to get away from home and he really wanted to study sculpture abroad. He said there were no really good sculpture schools then in the United States. He did admire the work of his teacher, George Grey Barnard, and he liked Eakins, but he felt that Europe was the place to learn. Jacob was truly a freethinker and did not believe in marriage, which my father could not understand.

Jacob had a very lovely girl. Her name was Adele Rabinowitz, and she was a schoolteacher on the Lower East Side. Jacob did not want to marry her. He wanted to live common law with her. She went to my mother and she told her that Jacob didn't want to marry her, but he wanted to live with her contract marriage. My mother said: "Don't you dare live contract marriage. He doesn't want to marry you? Let him keep away from you." When Jacob left for Europe in 1902 he kept in touch with Adele. Then, you know, he was suffering – he was very sick in Paris. Adele went over to meet him; she was in love with him. He was in very bad straits and he came back home for his first visit, in 1905. They missed each other and never married.

Jacob loved the Lower East Side. Even though my mother and father had come from Poland, they were more Americanized than most people there, for almost all were European or Russian Jews, very orthodox. My mother and father spoke Polish, Russian, Yiddish and English. My mother and father spoke Yiddish to each other and my mother spoke Yiddish to the different people but never to me.

When my parents didn't want us to understand what they said they would speak Polish and Russian, not Yiddish, because we children all understood it. We heard Yiddish out on the street, Hester Street. Downtown everybody spoke Yiddish, but my parents spoke four languages.

My grandmother Lena was not Americanized. She came to live in New York City and she wanted to die in Poland. My dad paid for her to cross the Atlantic thirteen times, as she was trying to die there. She didn't die in Poland though, but in the United States.

People on the Lower East Side believed in the Evil Eye. I remember my brother-in-law, Jacob Stone, Ida's husband. When his children were small and anyone would look at them, he'd go: "Phht. Phht. Phht." Three times back and forth. He'd spit and say: "That takes the curse off the Evil Eye." He was a very religious man. Everyone down there believed in the Evil Eye, Chinese, Italian, Jews, Europeans. When something good comes, something bad comes along with it. A beautiful child is likely to be cursed. I remember that. The Evil Eye. . . funny.

Nobody but my grandmothers, Sarah and Lena, wore wigs. However, every week my mother, my sisters Ida and Chana, went to the ritual baths, the *mikvah*. My sister Ida even went when we lived in Harlem. Not me. I didn't even go when I was married. Ahhh – to me it was silly. I felt emancipated. I'm going to go to a *mikvah*? I was a rebel. I never went.

We used to go to the Beach in Coney Island. Jacob wrote me in one of his last letters that he missed the beaches living in England. It is too cold there for ocean bathing. When he and his son Jackie visited his daughter Peggy Jean at Cape Hatteras after the war, he wrote me of his pleasure on the beaches there. He said it was his first vacation in fifty years. Jacob didn't always tell the truth; that was an exaggeration, but he didn't have such beaches in England. Coney Island was a lot of fun. Oh, it was crowded, crowded with people. They'd let us wade in the water. I had a bathing suit, not like I have today, but with a skirt and stockings, you know.

My mother and my sister Ida would sit on the beach and watch us. We'd go with Ida's children, Florence and Danny Stone. These people, Nathan's, had a place where you used to sit down and my sister Ida was a very rich woman. So we'd all go in and sit down and have a hot dog and a drink, cream soda, two cents plain, or something like that. I only wanted the red soup and they didn't know what the hell the red soup was. It was clam chowder and my family was Kosher. I only wanted the red soup, and so they'd say: "Get her the red soup." My mother didn't eat it, so she never knew it was clam chowder. For me she got it. I think it was five or ten cents for a bowlful. Only the red soup – get her the red soup. Oh, it was delicious.

Did I go on the rides? Did I? I rode the Shoot the Chutes and they had another place where you'd go down into the water. This is funny, I went into the place, I don't remember the name of it now, but it was famous. We got into the boats and there was a woman on it who had on a gold necklace. The fellow who was towing and standing in the back pulled the necklace off. I saw it. When we got out, she said: "My necklace is gone."

I said: "He took it." He threw it in the water and ran away. I believe that was on the Shoot the Chutes. Oh, we went into the Tunnel of Love and everything. I rode them all. How I used to love those places.

My father was very religious, very orthodox. Max Epstein was president of the *shul* on Forsythe. He built the *shul*, for he put up most of the money. He was very easy with money, just like Jacob. That was one of the reasons why they didn't get along – they were alike. The *shul* was very orthodox. The men sat separate and the women sat separate. The women sat upstairs in the balcony and the men sat downstairs. You know ten men make up a *minyan* and they can form a *shul*. They don't need a rabbi. They can perform all religious duties set up by the *Torah*. Orthodox Jews live their religion every day. It starts when they get up in the morning. They begin the day with a prayer and have prayers through the day. Some of them would lay *tefillim*, the leather prayer straps. They would put them on their head, bring it around and lay on their arms. All my brothers got this kind of religious training.

CHAPTER THREE

Jacob went alone to Paris in 1902. We went down to see him off on the boat. On the ship was the Volks' son, Jake Volk. The Volks owned a big delicatessen downtown, on the Lower East Side. It was a business like the Isaac Gellis people had, the same kind of deal. I remember I stood there, a child, and my mother saw Jake Volk. Jake Volk was a pretty fast fellow, especially with women. My mother said: "Oh, my God, my son. He's going with *Jake Volk.* My God, he's going in bad company."

My mother was crying. I stood there, looking at her. My mother's crying. Why is she crying? He's going on the boat. He's going to Europe.

Jacob was twenty-two years old when he went to Paris and to the *École des Beaux-Arts.* He shared rooms in Montparnasse with Bernard Gussow but his money soon ran out. My mother got Ida and Lou, both of whom were well-off, to send him seventy-five dollars a month allowance. She used to bother Ida and Lou. "Did you send Jacob money orders?" The two of them used to chip in every two weeks and send him money. They'd say:

"Yes, Mother, we'll send 'im, we'll send 'im." This is funny, but an artist by the name of Noble* was in Paris then and he came back and told us later that the minute Jacob got the money all the artists who didn't eat would gather round. He would pay off his room rent and bills and then buy them all food and drink, or whatever they had. Ida and Lou didn't know this at the time. My father never sent him any money at all.

So, at the *Beaux-Arts* – ah, he used to have a habit when he would try and make something. They'd have a model in front of the class and he'd run up to measure. He said: "They would sit back," (he told me this) "they would sit back and make whatever they wanted, but I was intent on getting *exactly* what I wanted so I would run up every minute to the figure and measure it and come back." Then he would cover the sculpture up for the night and when he would come back in the morning it would be in pieces. The other students destroyed it, so he stopped the study there and he went to Julian's. There the teachers called him the American Indian, you know?

I remember when he came home after mother died; it must have been in 1927. When Jacob was first studying he used to make *maskeri* – old faces, monsters, caricatures, we'd call them *grotesquerie* today. My mother hung a *maskeri* on the wall, and all his drawings she kept in a trunk. So when he came back, he said to me: "I had some drawings – what happened to them?"

"Well," I said, "they threw them out after mother died." Things like that happened to Jacob's work. After Peggy Jean and her first husband, Norman Hornstein, were divorced, Norman took as a settlement a major share of the Epstein work which he and Peggy Jean owned. He was the boss. He moved to Syracuse to be near his daughter, and the house he was living in burned down. All the Epstein drawings and paintings were destroyed. There were nudes and drawings of Jackie, Epstein's son. Peggy Jean now has work by her father which is mostly of her family, such as Margaret Epstein, her children, and herself. That was the way it was with Jacob's work. His studios burned down, people ridiculed and vandalized his work and some of it just disappeared.

In 1905 Lou and Ida were tired of sending Jacob money in Europe and so they sent him a ticket to come home. Jacob was then in desperate straits, so he returned. It was the time when my sister Honey was to be married. When Jacob got off the boat he was wearing open sandals, no stockings, open shirt and terrible pants, and he had long hair, dressed Buster Brown fashion. My sister Honey,

---

*Probably Thomas Satterwaite Noble (1835-1907) an American painter who had been a Confederate officer in the American Civil War. He studied under Couture in Paris, and painted miscegenation in America

who was near in age and a favorite companion, walked with him. She went with him to the park. My father was very upset. He said: "What is this? Everybody thinks he's crazy."

When Jacob heard of Honey's engagement he was very upset. She was to marry Joe Solomon, no relation to us. Joe was a butcher down on the Lower East Side. Almost everyone disliked the match, except my father. Ida and Jacob Stone were very unhappy about it. Joe Solomon also invested in real estate, as well as being a butcher. I guess Chana liked the match. Chana, Honey, she was a doll. Her picture in her beautiful engagement dress is the one I picked for this book. My father, you see, arranged most of the marriages for his children and he looked for wealth for his daughters. He couldn't arrange my marriage, but he did most of them. He knew all the business people around on Hester and Forsythe Streets. Jacob Stone, Ida's husband, was a very wealthy man who had a fabrics store on Hester called *Jacob Stone & Brother*. Mrs. Stone, his mother, had a cafe on Eldridge.

Ida had as a young girl been engaged to Charlie Gellis of the Isaac Gellis people and one night Charlie came to take her out. My mother was very sick after labor. I think she had just had me. Ida said: "My mother is very sick. I am not going out."

Charlie said: "All right. I'll go around the corner and take out your cousin." Ida got very angry. She took off the diamond earrings he had given her and the diamond ring, and she threw them down the stairs. I don't know if they ever found them or not. She didn't marry for many years after that. It was a disgrace then not to marry and she was considered an old maid. She married Jacob Stone at about twenty-four. Charlie Gellis married his cousin and a funny thing is that she lives near me now in New York. I see her in the park and she says to me:

"I'm not a bit surprised that your sister threw him over. He was overbearing. He was very hard to get along with."

* * * * * *

Jacob only stayed two weeks in 1905 and then he went back to Europe, to London I think, because my father made life so miserable for him. He did not return to the United States again until 1927. My mother cried and cried when he left, saying that she would never see him again, and she was right. She died in 1913.

All the children began to marry. Ida Stone and her husband had three children, Florence Holly, who is one of several Florences in our family (her married name is Holly), Danny, who died recently, and Irving Stone.

My brother Lou was a very quiet, refined young man. He worked with my father and he married Deena Grozcky, the landlord's daughter at 1661 Madison Avenue, where we lived. Lou and Deena had four children: Ethel Evans, who died some time ago — she was an artist and did designs for fabrics, etc., — the cartoonist Abner Dean, Irving Evans, who worked as stage manager and treasurer for Radio City Music Hall, and Mickey Herbert, a very beautiful girl. Abner is very talented, a fine artist. I understand he is doing sculpture and architectural work. Abner took the name of his mother for his last name and Irving took Evans.

Chana and Joe Solomon had five children: Harriet, Jerry, both of whom died recently, Irving, Mickey and Florence.*

Hyman Epstein never had any children for he was unmarried and died of peritonitis at twenty-seven years of age. Although I married Alexander Press, I, too, never had any children.

Harold Epstein had two children. He married Naomi Schnitzer and his children are Leonard Epstein and Marthe Epstein Clamage, a sculptor and teacher. She is helping me write this book.

Dr. Irving Epstein died in 1978. He and his wife Leah had two children: Dr. Howard Evans, professor of zoology at Cornell University, and Dr. Martin Evans, a pediatrician. They too took the

---

*Florence Solomon died in 1981 and Abner Dean in 1982.

name of Evans because my brother said they should. He said he had a lot of trouble; he was in the army in World War I and he spoke French beautifully. In fact, he used to teach French in the army. They used to say to him: "You're a hell of a big Jew. You know, Epstein, you're a hell of a big Jew." My brother was over six feet tall. And he had a hard time in the army because he was a Jew. He didn't change his name, but when his sons went to college, he made them change theirs. They didn't want to change it. They said if it was good enough for Jacob Epstein, it was good enough for them.

Jacob had many children, among whom are Peggy Jean, Jackie, and Kitty. I think he accepted the other two, Theo and Esther, but Margaret Epstein did not.

Some of the Epstein grandchildren are also artists. My niece Marthe has a son, Marc Clamage, who is an artist. Marshall Stone, Ida's grandson is a movie producer. We are a family of artists.

Plate 1: 102 Hester Street, New York City: home of the Max Epstein family (photographed in 1976)

Plate 2: Hester Street, looking east from the corner of Ludlow Street (Photograph by Jacob A Riis), Jacob A Riis Collection, Museum of the City of New York

Plate 3: Hester Street, corner of Norfolk Street, Courtesy of The New York Historical Society, New York City

Plate 4: Hester Street, c1898, Courtesy of The New York Historical Society

Plate 5: Mary Solomon Epstein, c1890

Plate 6: Hester Street, north side of Clinton, c1900, U.S. History, Local History and Genealogy Division, The New York Public Library, Astor, Lenox and Tilden Foundations

Plate 7: Hester, Suffolk & Essex Streets (left foreground: Seward Park), April 10 1931 (photographer: P L Sperr), U.S. History, Local History and Genealogy Division, The New York Public Library, Astor, Lenox and Tilden Foundations.

Plate 8: (Clockwise from top left) Sarah Solomon, c1870; Lena Barntovsky, c1875; Max Epstein, c1880; Isaac Solomon, c1870

Plate 9: Harold and Sylvia Epstein, c1905

Plate 10: Jacob Epstein, 1907; Chana Epstein, 1905 (engagement photograph: detail of plate 11)

Plate 11: (Top left) Ida Epstein, c1895;
(top right) Louis Epstein, c1905;
(bottom) Chana Epstein, 1905 (engagement photograph)

Plate 12: Jacob Epstein, 1910 or 1912

CHAPTER FOUR

We moved quite a bit in New York after we left Hester Street. My father was among the first to move uptown. Our first place was 1661 Madison Avenue, between 110th and 111th Streets. We moved there in 1899 after Harold was born. This was a large, six-room apartment; it was a railroad flat. The neighborhood was lovely when we were there, brownstone houses with walkup flats, no elevators then. My brother Lou married the landlord's youngest daughter, Deena, whom he met while we lived there. They were married around 1905. My father was busy investing in real estate and in building; he had given up his grocery and bakery.

The first school I went to was at 111th Street, between Fifth Avenue and Lenox Avenue. The landlord's daughter, Rose, was very friendly with Ida and they had to take me to school. I shook like a leaf. I was so scared; I was nervous. I was about six years old. So, when they came home, they said: "Oh, my God in Heaven, I hope it's going to be all right. She was shaking like a leaf." The school lasted from nine o'clock in the morning until three in the afternoon. We went home for lunch and then came back. No one-room school – we had grades. I was very good in gymnastics and dancing, all that, and painting.

Ida had moved uptown with us but she married Jacob Stone around 1902 and went back to the Lower East Side to live, on Eldridge, at the corner of Hester. Simpson's, the pawnbrokers, were also on the corner, right next to Jacob Stone's fabrics store. We knew the Simpsons very well. Another person my family knew was Irving Berlin. Jacob Stone owned a lot of property uptown. He owned a building at 108th Street and Madison Avenue, and he bought the house at the corner of 118th and Madison Avenue. Jacob Stone also owned the apartment house at 119th Street and Lenox Avenue. It was a corner house and my brother Irving (we called him Doc) had his office there. Irving lived at Ida's for a while before he married.

I remember my mother used to send me downtown to Ida's on Eldridge Street when she lived there after her marriage. I would carry bowls of *gefiltefish* down to Ida and I would ride the Madison Avenue streetcars. I remember those cars. We'd take them, my mother, Ida, and all of us children. We'd go to Manhattan Beach. Do you know how long it took? Hours. Two hours or more, at least. My sister Ida at that time had two children and she used to carry her jewelery in her pocketbook. The pocketbook fell out of the streetcar once. She started screaming, so the people thought one of the children had fallen out. They stopped the streetcar and ran back two blocks. She showed 'em the purse. The conductor said: "If I'd known you had jewelery in there I'd never of stopped." I was a child but I remember that distinctly. How I remember those streetcars. Everyone stood on the running board. When it was crowded, the men stood on the running board, some women too, but mostly men. You could fall right off; there was nothing to hold onto.

We had horsecars at 110th Street and Fifth Avenue, horse-drawn trolleys. There were no subways then. Elevateds – they had those for a long time – one on Third Avenue, one on Second, and one on the West Side at Eighth Avenue. I'd ride the L – you could look right down into the houses because the elevated was so near the houses and the windows of the houses were open. We used to shop at *Siegel's and Cooper,* a department store on Sixth Avenue and Twenty-third Street. They were the first to give Sperry green stamps.

The Epstein boys swam in the East River. It wasn't polluted then like it is now. My brother Irving used to swim there. They had wooden barges anchored in the river and where they were anchored marked off the swimming area. The swimmers would rent lockers on the barges for a few pennies.

My brother Louey was a rent collector down on the East Side, in Chinatown, for some very rich people. Max Epstein made him carry a gun when he collected the rents. Lou was a very quiet young man. He collected rents, he was in real estate with my father, he did everything. My father was wealthy then; that's why when people used to say that Jacob came from a poor family, Jacob would get very angry. He would get so mad. "My parents are not poor people" he'd say. When my father was doing construction he would make a lot of money, so he took and gave to my mother one hundred thousand dollars. He told her to save it; it was for their future. All of a sudden in 1907 the Panic came and he had to pay back the mortgages. One of the men who had mortages on his houses was a man by the name of Mandel. Mandel, we knew them very well, and it was either pay them or go into bankruptcy. My father would not go into bankruptcy so he took the hundred thousand dollars from my mother.

She said: "That's all we got and you're getting older. You'll never, never come back. Why are you taking this money from me?"

"I made it," he said. "I gave it to you; I'll make it again." But he never came back after that. Never came back at all.

So what did he do? I understand he went to his children and got help; he was always doing that. We all helped him in his old age. When he asked Jacob for money one time, Jacob offered him ten dollars. After the 1907 Panic he opened another grocery store and sold fancy delicatessen items to the wealthy families. We lived in 1907 at 8 West 114th Street, on the first floor. Jacob Stone owned that house. We moved down to 83rd Street and Lexington Avenue. It was a wooden house and we had a shop on the first floor. We lived upstairs. Oh, it was a very exclusive neighborhood. The ladies didn't come into the store; they sent their butlers to shop. We sold to the carriage trade.

I went then to P.S. Six at Madison Avenue and 85th Street. It's gone now; they've built a big apartment house where it was. That was like a private school; the elite went there, all the children of the rich. I used to play hookey and go over to the Metropolitan Museum. I practically lived there; that's why I know so much about the Metropolitan. It was lovely – all open air around the museum. The museum showed Rodin's work and the picture galleries were beautiful.

Now they have my brother's work in the basement. Rodin, Epstein, everything good is in storage. The curator wrote me, a Jewish fellow, he'd like to come and see what I've got. He said if I wanted to see my brother's work they'd take me down to see it. I didn't answer him. I know my brother's work will come back. He was an extraordinary artist.

When Jacob went back to Europe he married his first wife, Margaret Gilmour Dunlop. He had met her while he was studying in Paris. He used to visit in Paris at the home of a man who was an anarchist. His name was Victor Dave and he had been in prison for being an anarchist. Margaret visited at the house too. She was a writer, living in Paris and writing. She also was an anarchist. Jacob got very sick during this time and Margaret nursed him; she felt sorry for him. In 1906 Jacob married her, out of gratitude for her care. It had been because of her that they went to London. She thought he would do better there.

Margaret was a Scotswoman. We all called her Peggy. I understand she had been married before she married Jacob. She had been married to a lord and divorced, I hear. She was a very bright, intellectual woman. She was tall and heavy, and she was ten, twelve, or fifteen years older than Jacob. Margaret was some woman. My brother Jacob didn't appreciate her. She gave up her writing, all of it, after she married Jacob. She did everything only for Jacob. She gave up everything, only to be what Jacob wanted. She was always madly in love with him.

Margaret knew everybody of importance in London. She helped Jacob get the Medical Association Building commission in the London Strand. His bid was the cheapest and through her efforts he got it. The trouble was that she was so much older than Jacob and she never had any children. I understand she couldn't, although she never did discuss why she couldn't with me. Well, he got the Strand commission and he had Peggy to help him as a mother does, for he was a dreamer. He was absent-minded, caring nothing for monetary encouragement. He truly loved art and the creating of it. He was busy studying at the British Museum, all that great art there, and trying to get established. The furore that the eighteen Strand figures, *The Ages of Man*, caused was great. People wanted him to take them down, to drape them. They didn't like the pregnant woman and the nude old woman; they called them obscene. Jacob had done research for these figures and he knew what he wanted; his mind was made up. He loved the natural and disliked the sham, the artificial. Primitive, simple types appealed to him. He defended his work and his fame spread.

Margaret was helping him in every way. She arranged for shows, for commissions; she ran his house and paid all the bills. She also kept the books and did a lot of the correspondence. Jacob was free to pursue his art. Why, he didn't even carry money. Never had a cent in his pocket. I remember when I visited them in 1928, Margaret had a big drawstring bag in which she carried money. She would take it out and do the paying, even at the Café Royal. Jacob would take a cab; he loved riding in cabs, and he would not have any money to pay the driver. The driver would come to the door at 18 Hyde Park Gate and say: "Mrs. Epstein, it's this – or that", and she would give him the fare. All the drivers knew him.

Jacob began to get commissions to do portraits. In this way he supported himself and his family, for famous people began to sit for him. Many people were afraid of his portraits. He never flattered anybody, but only modelled what he saw in the face and soul. Some did not want this much laid bare, yet they were curious. The sitter had to interest Jacob in order for him to do the portrait, no matter what the price was. He always preferred to pay someone to sit for him who interested him and would inspire him to do the unusual.

He was a young, virile sculptor, and he was very honest, not at all polished. He was called "The Stormy Petrel", and being a Jew was also against him. It kept him from getting many commissions. However, around 1909 Jacob got the Oscar Wilde Tomb commission for the grave of Wilde in Père Lachaise Cemetery in Paris. He researched it and worked on it a long time and in 1912 it was completed and shipped across the Channel to Paris. He went there to install it and while he was there he met Picasso, Brancusi and Modigliani. He was good friends with all of them. Picasso and Jacob went to an exhibition together in London. Jacob told me that people were always trying to get him in dutch with Picasso, to try to start something between the two.

Jacob lived near Modigliani in Paris in 1912. Modigliani was a dope fiend and a drunkard. My brother used to feel sorry for him. There were people there who were intent on making something out of Modigliani's failings. They had him stuck in a basement and they would give him drugs and drink. He'd make sketches and things. My brother tried to help him. He got him out of there. Jacob had a drawing by Modigliani in the studio of his house in London. Modigliani had given it to him.

The Oscar Wilde Tomb sculpture was put up in the Père Lachaise Cemetry in 1912 and the Prefect of Police refused to let it be unveiled unless Jacob altered it. It was a nude sculpture of a flying male demon angel and it showed the sex organs. Jacob got very angry. He threatened to demolish the features of the Prefect's face if he touched the sculpture. Jacob was arrested, since he wouldn't let the police near it, but he had defenders of his work and they interceded. Finally it was unveiled, but a metal plate had been attached to cover the sex organs.

Jacob could breathe life like a soul into stone, so naturally he had many people jealous of him. He was also very exacting in his choice of materials. The materials had to be perfect and this cost money. Whatever he received in payment for his commission was soon absorbed into another work. In 1910 Jacob did his first abstract piece, *Sunflower*, and he also started the first *Sun God*. In 1913-1915 he did the last abstract piece, *The Rock Drill*. Jacob didn't like abstractions much. He told me that he was through with abstraction. "I don't like it," he said. "I am *through* with it. I am finished with it." Anybody who did abstract art he had no use for.

Jacob also said that there were no good sculptors here in America. He didn't like any of them. He did admire the Borglum monuments on Mount Rushmore. He thought that was very good.

On February 1 1913 Mary Epstein died. Jacob told me about his dream of her. He said: "Isn't it funny that I should dream of Mother, that she wasn't there anymore, and then to hear later that she died?" That's all he ever said about the dream.

CHAPTER FIVE

While Jacob was attracting such attention in Europe I was going to school. Harold was a small child. Irving was finishing up school and beginning to study medicine. My brother Hyman, or Hymie, had become a problem to our family. The family considered him to be a very bad boy because he got interested in Catholicism. Hymie only went around with Irish Catholic boys; they were all his friends. Oh, Hymie was handsome, handsome. He had red hair; he was blue-eyed, and he was a typical Irishman. I was told that Hymie converted to Catholicism. That to my father was poison. Max Epstein thought that there was something wrong with Hymie. "He's not all there," said my father, "if he could believe in Catholicism." My father would have nothing to do with Hymie. Hymie left the family. I was quite young when it happened. My mother would sometimes take me with her when she visited Hymie. She would visit him on Saturdays and take him food. He was in a large room; I thought my father must have had Hymie put away, where it was, I didn't know. Hymie would pick me up and carry me around in his arms. He was tall, well-built, and such a good-looking man.

All of a sudden Hymie got appendicitis and peritonitis set in. They notified my mother that he was sick and then that he had died at East Islip, Long Island, on May 29, 1909. My mother was so upset. She cried and cried, so bitterly. Hymie was buried by my parents in Washington Cemetery in Brooklyn. He is not buried with my mother and father, but over on the new side. I remember how my mother cried and cried. She was hysterical.

My mother was a big, heavy woman and she had heart trouble. A year or two before her death I went to live at my sister Ida's. She and Jacob Stone lived then at 118th Street and Lenox Avenue, in Harlem. A lot of important Jewish families lived around there. The famous actor, Jacob Adler, lived around the corner from us, on Lenox Avenue. I used to see him all the time on the street. He was a very nice looking man, but he was old. He was very distinguished-looking, with nice features. He was grey-haired and he had a long face with a long nose. He dressed expensively and he looked something like the *Majestas* that Jacob Epstein made for Llandaff Cathedral. Adler's wife Sarah was also a famous actress, and he has very well-known children, Stella and Luther Adler. Now Jacob Adler loved women. Ah, he was a great one for young girls. I remember I was a young girl at the time. He never approached me, though.

The Gellers, the shoe people, had a store near Lenox Avenue. Murray Geller, the son, used to call me up and I used to make believe I wasn't home when I answered the phone. I didn't like him. I'd say: "She's not home."

He'd say: "I know she's home and it's you talking."

Another famous family who lived around there were the Cohns. I never knew Harry Cohn, who became head of Columbia Pictures, but his family lived near us in Harlem. I knew Harry's brother, Harvey, and I knew his brother Clarence. I used to go out with Clarence. We were friends.

When I was a young girl living on 118th Street I used to know the girl who was living then with Joseph Schenck. She was a lovely girl, the one he was keeping, and he was stuck on her. She was a nice Jewish girl. He went with a lot of Gentile girls later and he married that Talmadge girl, but this was before that. I was then around fifteen years old, and one day I saw them coming down the street. He stopped, and I ran away. My family was very strict with me and I was afraid of getting my name in the papers. I was *scared*. Joseph Schenck used to live around there, then.

Benny Leonard, the famous Jewish fighter, lived on Fifth Avenue. His mother lived on Fifth

Avenue. I knew him. He was a little fellow. He wasn't fat. He was a lightweight, and a good looking man. He was a fancy dresser, in the way of prize fighters. Sometimes he'd wear a sweater – or something like that. I wasn't supposed to be out with him, but once he and his friend Cummings took me to a fight at Madison Square Garden. Leonard was fighting. We got within two blocks of the Garden and I said: "Oh, you'd better let me out here because if my family knows I'm going to a fight with Benny Leonard, I'll get killed – I'll get murdered at home." You see, they were very strict.

Benny said: "Don't worry. We won't tell."

I said: "Don't let me go in with you." His friend Cummings and I went into the fights. Oh, I'm telling you, I started to cry. The fights were – there was blood and everything. They fought with gloves. Oh, it was terrible.

While I lived on 118th Street I used to have dresses made by Madame Nemser. I'm still friendly with her sister. She calls me up all the time. Madame Nemser had a dressmaking business before she became a famous designer. She married a Mr. Nemser, who was in the candy business. He was a good businessman and they went into wholesale – *Nemser's Dresses*. Before that she used to do her own dressmaking, and she dressed me. She was a pretty, blonde woman of medium height, and she had a pleasant personality. I had a beautiful figure and she said: "It's a pleasure to make something for her. She walks out; she looks like a million dollars."

I remember Fifth Avenue on Easter Sunday. The men all used to wear high hats, all dressed up, oh, yes, with canes. The women were dressed up tight, with bodices. One Easter, I was about sixteen or seventeen, I was walking on Fifth Avenue and they took my picture. It came out in the Rotogravure of *The New York Times*. I had on a taffeta suit with a hat. You never went out without a hat and gloves, white gloves.

One day I was walking on Fifth Avenue and I had on a black velvet coat, fitted tight. I had a nice, busty figure and the coat was double-breasted, with pearl buttons. It was a stunning outfit, and along comes what's his name – Enrico Caruso. And he's flirting with me – giving me the wink. I'm getting scared; I know who he is, you know, from his pictures in the paper. I'm frightened stiff, and all the while he's giving me the wink, the nod. He wants to talk to me. I'm a young girl, and, you know, in the Monkey House at the Zoo, at 60th some-odd Street, he molested a girl. The girl got scared and they wanted to arrest him.

Before my mother died, I graduated from P.S. Six. Mother died right after I graduated. I remember when I graduated I went around to all my teachers with my book for them to sign. They liked me. One of my teachers used to make me show the other students how to do gymnastics, because I was so good in athletics. When I went to Mr. Pyser, one of the teachers, to sign my autograph book, he said: "At last you've come to me, to sign your book." I was a gay person, always singing and dancing and people all liked me.

My mother was afraid of this; she was afraid I'd get into trouble being so friendly and nice.

I was around fourteen of fifteen years old and I was an attractive girl. The fellows got interested in me. There was one man who lived in a private house on 118th Street. We lived on the corner. He came from a millionaire's family, and he was after me. His family was in woolens. He said to me: "Why don't you let me go out with you? Why don't you come and see me?" One fellow who was interested in me thought I was an older girl.

"I don't want you using lipstick", he told me.

"Don't tell me what to do", I said. He found out I was fifteen years old and he dropped me like a hot potato. He was a man of about thirty. That was an old man to me. I can't remember his name but he was a nice fellow. He had a haberdashery store on Broadway and 66th Street. Mostly I went out with Jewish boys. It was a *disgrace* to go out with Gentiles, and to marry? Later, when I was in the garment industry I'd go out with Gentiles if they were buyers, or something like that. It was for business though, luncheon and dinner dates, things like that.

About this time the actor Thomashevsky was very popular. He was big and fat and very attractive to girls. There was a story told about him, that he had an affair with a woman and later she had twins. The people wanted the actor to divorce his wife and marry the woman, to help bring up the twins, but he flatly refused.

I loved the stage. I wanted to go on it. My mother was so scared I'd end up on the stage. That, too, was a disgrace, to have actors and actresses in the family. All my singing and dancing frightened my mother. She didn't like anything pertaining to the stage. Well, I was tall, with a wasp waist and I had a big bust. Everyone said: "Look at her waistline", I used to be ashamed of my big bust and I would try to flatten it, try to cover it up . . . almost ruined myself. And I tried to go on the stage. It happened while my mother was still alive. A Mr. Lee wanted to put me on the stage at The Winter Garden. He was the husband of a headliner, Eva Shirley. She was a singer and she appeared at The Palace Theater. Mr. Lee wanted me to go into the chorus at the Winter Garden and I refused. I said: "I want a part".

They all laughed. They said: "Everybody starts in the chorus". I refused; I wouldn't start in the chorus. My family wouldn't have let me anyway. They were very strait-laced.

Then my mother got very sick with heart trouble. She had insurance from the *landsman* and she went up to Lebanon Hospital where my brother Irving was interning. He was training to be a general practitioner. My mother was fifty-five years old and she was dying. Ida brought me to see her. Mother couldn't speak. She was pointing to me and she was pointing to my sister Ida, that she should take care of me. Ida was saying to her: "Don't worry, Ma, I'll take good care of her. I'll see that nothing happens to her." I remember that so distinctly. I can see it now.

After mother died my father moved in 1913 up to an apartment at 112th Street near Lenox Avenue. They were scared to have me in a household with men and I shouldn't have a woman in the house – my mother. So I continued to live with my sister Ida – my sister was some watchdog. *That* was a *watchdog.* Harold lived with his father except for two years when he got rheumatic fever and went to live at Ida's, where she took care of him. Irving also lived at Ida's for a short while before he married.

In rich Jewish families the daughters did not work. It was a disgrace to have a daughter who worked. They didn't want me to work, but *I wanted to work.* After my mother died, I went out and got a job. My sisters didn't work; they got married. As I said, my father made the matches. He arranged Chana's and Ida's marriages and they had to marry whom he wanted. He was very money concious. I was unusual and later my father was very proud of me. Single girls weren't doing what I was doing; my sisters weren't doing what I did. I went out with a group of girls from P.S. Six after our graduation. We went to look for a job in the garment center, into a building on Thirty-fifth Street. The name of the firm was *The Crescent Dress Company.* We were all on the elevator and a girl got on. She said to us: "No need looking, they're all filled". A woman was standing near the elevator and she saw me. She was the owner and she said to me:

"Young lady, are you looking for a position as a model?" I said yes. She said: "Come off, come off the elevator."

I got off and she said: "Did you ever work before?"

I said: "No, never."

She said: "Well, come in." She took me into the firm and they started fitting dresses on me. They fitted me like they were poured on me. I was busty; I had the figure, with the big bust and the waistline. I had an eighteen-inch waistline. You can see it in my pictures. I wore a girdle, never wore a corset. So I went to work there as a model. They had then two steady models, a blonde and a brunette. I was in between, a reddish blonde. I worked there for five weeks. The woman trained me, showed me how to walk and to turn around. She said: "It's a short season, only five weeks." Before the five weeks was up I went to another coat and suit house. I was there the whole season.

They had thirty-five girls, and I, and another girl, were asked by all the salesmen to model for their customers because we were good models. Her name was Sylvia too. She was a brunette and I was the strawberry blonde. I was very friendly. Models were picked for their hair coloring and how you filled out the garment. *I* filled out a garment. It helped to have a nice complexion. I had that, and I was good-looking. A lot of the models were good-looking, but you didn't have to be pretty. Some of the models who were juniors, the little sizes, weren't pretty. I was a misses model, size fourteen. Misses sizes ran from ten to twenty, and then they had the mature woman sizes, the half sizes.

From that company I went to work at *The Wonder Dress Company*. I stayed there a long time and at first I modelled for them. I used to have a cheap dressmaker who'd make my own clothes for me. She'd make a dress for me for about six dollars, and I'd tell her that I'd want this or that on it, and she would do it. I'd wear these clothes to work and everyone would admire them. So, at Wonder Dress the woman who did the designing was the wife of the man who owned it. She had been a schoolteacher, and her father had owned the place, but she had married one of the men there. She'd say to me: "Sylvia, how should I make this?" and I'd say: "Put this here", or "do that there". She'd do it and the garment would sell. One day I went one place on a job and I was riding the elevator. I have got on this gorgeous outfit which I had the dressmaker make up for me, and I'd designed it. It was black broadcloth with long sleeves, and it had a circular sleeve lined in red, fixed so the red lining showed. I can see it like it was today. A woman in her forties gets on the elevator. She is looking at my outfit. She says: "Young lady, who made that dress? Are you a designer?" She was a very well-known designer.

I said: "No, I'm not a designer. I'm looking for a modelling job."

She said: "Well, you should be a designer." So I told her that I went to a cheap dressmaker and told her what to do. She said to me: "You should design."

At Wonder Dress I would go around to all the stores and look at the different dresses. If I saw a dress that appealed to me, I'd come back to my boss or the designer and tell them, say that they could do this or that. I also sketched a little, and I was very handy with the fancy work, like bows and things. I'd make the bows and that would go on the dress. I was getting sixty-five dollars a week then and that was a very big sum of money for those days. My boss sent me out to sell, and I sold. So he said he'd give me two per cent extra. My salary then came to $250 a week. My boss said he didn't figure it right. He said: "I'll give you one and a half per cent." So I'd take home $125, $150 a week. That was a lot of money in those days. I would model the dresses and sell them at the same time. They would all ask for Sylvia Epstein, the buyers, and the salesmen would want me to wear the clothes. I was very well-liked.

I was living at Ida's and I paid nothing for room and board, so I had most of my salary for myself. We didn't have the taxes we have today. You could make money then; today the government takes all of it, almost. My sister Ida was a very rich woman; she didn't need it. She thought of me more as a daughter rather than as a sister. People would say: "Your blonde daughter" – meaning me, and she never would say anything. In fact, Florence, her daughter, used to say to me: "Mother likes you better than she does me."

Harold grew up and became a dentist. My brother Doc took him in with him in his apartment building. In fact, when Doc got married, he insisted on an eight-room apartment so that Harold could live with Leah and him, and open his dentist's office in the building. Doc had his medical office in the same building.

World War One came and my brother Doc went off to the army. We heard very little about Jacob. My sister Ida was very upset and worried. "There's something wrong with Jacob," she'd say. "They don't show his hands."

Jacob had gone into the British Army in 1917, but through the efforts of Queen Mary and others he was honorably discharged in 1918. Jacob was not mentally suited to be a soldier.

CHAPTER SIX

In 1918 Peggy Jean, Jacob's first daughter, was born. Her mother was the model for the *Meum* sculptures and her name was Meum Lindsell-Stewart. Dancers, showgirls, typists, maids – Jacob's models were taken from all walks of life and most of the women were very anxious to pose for him. Margaret did not seem to mind; she was not jealous, and *encouraged* all types of women to come to his studio. Jacob liked the natural, unpainted, and exotic type of woman. When I was there in 1928 Margaret told me; "If you see anyone who is exotic, tell her to come to the studio." Margaret knew all about the model-mistresses. He had a great number of mistresses, but few could hold his attention for long. He had a commune. The models would become part of the household. They lived there and their children did also. When the models became pregnant, they were sent to Paris, where the children were born. Margaret was on good terms with almost all of them. Jacob would do sculptures of all of them, and the model he was interested in at the time would be available at all times, since she lived in the house. He would study her manner, her attitudes, and moves. Margaret usually took her models under her wing, as a mother would.

Margaret Epstein never had any children at all. Meum Lindsell-Stewart was sent to Paris and she had Peggy Jean there. Margaret appealed to her there and asked her to give up the baby. She agreed to do so, and Margaret brought the baby back as Jacob's and hers. Peggy Jean was brought up in the house as theirs. This was also the case in 1934 with the birth of Epstein's young son, Jackie. His mother was the model Isobel Nicholas. Jacob and Margaret didn't adopt the children; they just brought them up as theirs. Margaret was a very broadminded woman and she understood Jacob. He loved children. He dearly loved Peggy Jean; he was crazy about her. Naturally he was selfish; remember when he took the bread and rolls at eight years old? As a man he had affairs galore and he thought first of his own needs. He thought of the artist first.

Everybody walked around the studio and house in the nude. It was very Bohemian. I never saw Margaret in the nude, but everybody else did it. They used to come and watch Peggy Jean bathe – she had such a lovely little body. I had trouble with Peggy Jean over this when she came over later to visit me. Their attitude was different, and they thought nothing of it. The morals of a genius are not to be judged in the same capacity as the ordinary layman's.

In the 1920's Meum Lindsell-Stewart became a Cochran Girl. He was a showman like Florenz Ziegfeld and he put on the same kind of extravaganza. I understand that the Meum later married very well. During the time that she modelled for Jacob she would come to see Peggy Jean. Peggy Jean told me that she remembered how she would pay attention to her, sometimes holding her and caressing her. She'd bring her toys and dolls, and she was the only one of the models who would do that. Peggy Jean didn't know she was her real mother. Margaret told her that when she was grown up and ready to be married. She also told her then about Jackie and his mother. After a while the Meum didn't come anymore. She gave Peggy Jean up, and later she died.

Margaret mothered Jacob. In my opinion he treated her like a dog, but he respected her because she mothered him, and he stayed married to her because of that. I don't think he ever cared for her in the same way that she did for him. I know Peggy Jean told me that she used to say to her: "Oh, he's going to leave me. He's going to leave me."

Peggy Jean would say to her: "Oh, Mummy, if he hasn't left you by now, he'll never leave you." Peggy Jean also told me that after Margaret died in 1947 she found letters written between Margaret and Jacob. "Aunt Sylvia," she said, "they weren't like letters between sweethearts, or a husband and wife. They were like letters between a brother and a sister."

Margaret took care of all his needs. She brought up his children, although they had governesses for Peggy Jean and Jackie when they were older. Margaret was everything Jacob needed. She looked a little like my mother; she was heavy, and she was sweet like my mother. In fact, when my father visited them in England, he came back and told me: "She looks like your mother. She reminds me of your mother." Margaret was a Scotswoman and Scotswomen are very clever, too. Margaret was a conniver, though, some conniver; I had trouble with her over that later.

Dolores was one of Jacob's early models and she was excellent. She was a woman who lived a free and easy life. She had one affair right after another. I don't know if Jacob ever had an affair with her. He never said. He did say: "I had a lot of trouble with her." He said that, because she insisted once, when he was passing by her flat, he went in. "I was passing by ," he said, "and there she was dancing around in the nude." She would do the craziest things. She would pose in a barrel – nude. She – in Blackpool, you know? Jacob said there was no getting away from her.

In 1921 Jacob met Kathleen Garman, a lovely young Welsh girl of about twenty. She came to the studio and she was a model for Jacob, as well as other artists. Jacob and she were very attracted to each other. Jacob had a lot of loves; he went from one to another and he would soon drop them, but Kathleen he deeply loved. I've never seen Kathleen, but my niece Marthe has met her and told me about her. She says that she was very exotic-looking, with striking features, not tall, but giving the appearance of being tall. She looks like her portraits and she has a broad forehead with large eyes and mouth. She was physically very attractive.

Kathleen did not stay at the Epstein house like the others. Jacob established a second household for her, almost from the start. Although Margaret was on good terms with most of the other models and all the American relatives, Kathleen she did not like. Margaret was fat, older, and burdened with Jacob's business affairs as well as running the house, entertaining, and bringing up his children. She had dropsy and her legs would swell up with water. She couldn't go to the art exhibitions; she didn't have the time. Kathleen would go to them, circulate, and gather news for Epstein. She would come back and tell them all she had heard and seen. She was an excellent model and also an interesting companion.

Kathleen had her home in Chelsea and in 1924 Theodore was born. In 1927 Kitty, Epstein's second daughter, was born, and Esther was born in 1929. Margaret accepted only Kitty as Jacob's child. Jacob accepted and supported all three of them.

Money was always a problem with Jacob and his family. Around 1914 Jacob had begun his collection of African art. It grew into one of the finest collections in the world. He was also financing his monumental works, so Margaret and he tried selling his art through a patron. My brother had almost no money and he needed a patron. John Quinn would take Jacob's paintings and his sculpture and he would buy them for very little money. Then he would sell them for large amounts. He was making money on them, so my brother had a big fight with Quinn about it, and Quinn got very upset and said he was going to get even with Epstein. He was going to sell his whole collection of Jacob's work. He did sell it – all of it. John Quinn said he was through with Epstein; Epstein was through with him.

Jacob had no business acumen. He didn't know the value of a dollar. Dealers stole from him. Later those dealers took his *Adam* – they were an American and an Englishman. They also took a lot of his portrait busts and Jacob had to pay over $3,500 to get the busts back.

Jacob would buy African and Pre-Columbian art like mad. The minute he'd get any money, he'd buy those things. He had buyers looking for him – in Paris. He never went to Africa to buy. He had a magnificent collection of art; he loved art. Once during the latter part of his life the French Government was making a film on French Equatorial art and they used part of his collection. My

use his art in the film and he said nothing, he was happy to have it shown. Jacob was a terrible businessman.

* * * * * *

Gradually I got into designing at Wonder Dress. They made dresses in the popular-priced range, $10.75 to $16.75, retailing for $20 to $29.95. The dress would be designed and a model of it made up. Then the design would be sent out to contractors, who would make one up and send it back for corrections. After it was approved it would be tried out on the buyers. If the buyers liked it, the company owners would say: "We'll put it in the line". They'd show it and take orders for it, and if it continued to sell, they'd say: "That's a good number; we'll keep it in the line". A good design would be made for several seasons. I would model and sell the dress to the buyers. I'd walk around the room and I always had something to say to them. I was friendly and I'd say: "This dress can be worn backwards", or something like that. I got their attention. When I was selling I'd go to the office and get my dress; sometimes I'd wear it and sometimes I'd take a model along or show it in the hand. I also went to other houses, big houses, and I'd model their clothes at times. While I was on the job, I'd see their dresses and they might appeal to me. I'd go home and tell my boss; he'd call in the embroiderers. I'd tell them how it was made; I'd sketch it sometimes. They were very simple dresses but the embroidery on them was gorgeous. One little change you make, and it's a different dress.

There was a place in New York, where if you paid a hundred dollars you could go in and see Paris originals. Sometimes I'd do that and get ideas. I'd also look at fashion magazines such as *Barbier's*, *Falbalas* and *Fanfreluches*, and of course there was the rotogravure in the newspapers. All the society women would be dressed up in their opera or ballgowns. Then I'd go to the department stores and look at the dresses. Other times the fabric houses would send in their salesmen with samples for us to choose from and I'd pick a fabric, go to the stores and get ideas to make the fabric into a design. The fabric could also be selected for a design I had already in mind when I saw the material. I designed street clothes but never coats, evening gowns, furs, or things like that.

The famous designers were all the rage. There was Paul Poiret and Lucile, who was really a society woman named Lady Duff-Gordon. Her sister was the novelist Elinor Glyn, who wrote that *Three Weeks*. I used to read that book constantly. And the clothes were gorgeous, gorgeous – they had the loveliest things. I would design coats and furs for myself, and have them made up by people in the trade. I knew all the people and these were private dressmakers. I'd design and order it and they'd make it up specially. I also bought Vionnet dresses for myself. I bought them in New York, and I had three, one black, one green, and one grey – all satin. They fitted skin tight. I copied those for Wonder Dress and I would copy Paul Poiret. I never copied Jeanne Lanvin, but I loved Vionnet. Her clothes were beautiful and so were Poiret's. I made the hobble skirt, the wrap-around dress; they were popular for a very long time. I'd take part of a design. I'd use the Italian peasant design. We'd do basques, a lot of basques, with full skirts. We'd use a lot of printed silks for the skirts and sometimes the basques would be of silver lamé. Stunning outfits. Then we'd sometimes make things with machine lace; there was a house in New York which sold machine-made lace. Handmade lace like *Valenciennes* was much too expensive for us, but I did sheaths with machine lace – sometimes with a nude or a pink slip underneath. We made velvet skirts; we used batiste for blouses, and we used a lot of chiffons.

Around World War One we made draped skirts worn with a contrasting cummerbund and a very simple blouse. We also used *Chantilly* lace. This was bought from lace houses in New York and they imported it from France. I used to make a collar of lovely lace and put it on a very simple dress. I'd also use *Chantilly* lace and make whole sheaths out of it, lining the sheaths with matching colored silk. I would use the lace for bodices and sometimes I'd make a tunic of lace with sleeves half-way down, all over a beautiful harem skirt. We'd keep it simple though. In popular-priced dresses you couldn't get too high-style. We'd do our fancy dresses for afternoon dresses. Printed materials were very popular. They could be worn to tea, receptions, things like that. We had a basic line; we kept it for several seasons pretty much the same. There was a dress once owned by Isadora Duncan on display at the Metropolitan Museum of Art during the *American Women of Style* Exhibition.* I did dresses like that. It was a simple sheath with a hobble skirt, raglan sleeve and gold embroidery, mink-trimmed on the bottom of the skirt. We'd leave off the mink and use the machine embroidery, Schiffli embroidery. This was about 1919 when that style was popular. Do you know who used to sell Schiffli embroidery? Jacqueline Susann, who wrote *The Valley of the Dolls*. I bought from her when I had my own company. She used to come around with samples, not too outstanding looking a girl. She sold the embroidery to all the dress companies.

We also made lots of things with ruffles, daytime dresses with ruffled skirts and a ruffled short train, the Spanish influence. We also used appliqué; that was sent out to contractors, like the fancy trim which we put on a lot of things.

Most of the people working in the garment center were Jewish or Italian. The Jews ran the businesses, and the seamstresses and embroiderers were mostly Jewish and Italian. The Italian women did beautiful machine embroidery – the Schiffli we used. Most of the tailors were Jewish, some Italian, as were the cutters and pattern makers. A cutter was very important; so was a presser. If you knew how to cut and how to press you had a professional garment half made. The cutters, tailors, pressers and pattern makers were mostly all men. I wanted to learn to cut. Cutters made very good money, but I never did. I never studied to do any of the things I did. I had a knack for it. I just picked it up.

The men made big money in the garment industry. After World War One, some of them made $12,000, $15,000 a year, selling, and some made $20,000 a year. That was good then, with no taxes like we have now, and low overhead. The men resented me, selling and making money too. They'd resent it when I'd come into an office to sell. The buyers would pull me in, not leave me outside standing there like they'd do the men. The buyers were mostly women, and I was very well-liked. They'd say: "Come on, Sylvia, sit here." The men hated that.

There were a lot of women working in the garment industry. Most of them were married and helping their husbands, who worked there too. They were buyers, the women, and designers. One of my friends was the designer Hannah Troy. I knew her when she first started out, when she was married to her first husband, Al Hartman. I used to take her around with me when I'd go to sell. She was very nervous. My friend Eva Burke was a buyer at Diamond Brothers, and they had a lot of stores, six, I think. I took Hannah up there. Hannah says: "Oh, Sylvia, I'm afraid. I'm afraid."

I said: "What are you afraid of? They won't eat you. Don't be afraid. I'll introduce you to her (Eva) and you'll get business."

I took her over and Hannah showed some of her clothes. Eva gave her an order for 6,000 dresses. Hannah said: "Oh, thank you, Sylvia", and she used to call for me every day after that, I should take her places. We all sort of helped each other, you know.

Mollie Parnis was another designer I knew. She started out as a saleswoman, not a designer. She worked with her first husband, designing, and Mollie Parnis has wonderful designers. Today she's a millionairess, a very shrewd businesswoman.

Then there was Dave Schwartz, who was Jonathan Logan. Now, there was some conniver, if there ever was one. I used to be friendly with his sister, who was a buyer of children's wear. I also knew Henry Rosenfeld. My friend Eva's nephew worked for him for years. A good friend of my early days as a designer was Fannie Fox, whose brother was I.J. Fox of Fifth Avenue. Fannie was a saleswoman

*This exhibition was organised by Mrs. Diana Vreeland, Special Consultant to the Costume Institute, and ran from December 13, 1975-August 31, 1976.

and she and I had a lot of fun. She knew a lot of people, and we used to go places together, travel together a lot. I.J. Fox – they were millionaires.

I never knew Elisabeth Hawes or Mainbocher, or Claire McCardell. I met Adele Simpson and I knew her husband, who was in the textile business. I knew people who worked for Norell. In fact, one of the salesmen who worked for Norell worked for me in my own firm later. I never knew the Hollywood or French designers, although my sister-in law, Margaret Epstein, knew Captain Molyneux very well. When I was going to Paris, after visiting them, she told me to call on Molyneux and tell him I was the sister of Jacob Epstein. "He'll be very nice to you, Sylvia", she said to me. I didn't do it.

CHAPTER SEVEN

My brother Lou moved out to Yonkers with his family and became a commuter. He was one of the first to become a suburbanite, but we did a lot of visiting back and forth, for we are, and have always been, a very close family. At Ida's I was treated beautifully and I liked living there very much. My sister Ida was a wonderful woman, I'll say that for her. I was independant; I lived at home, and I was making good money. Now I've been a woman of the world. I've travelled a lot and done a lot of things, but I was never cheap or common. My sister saw to that.

I used to go to all the balls. Jacob and Ida Stone took me once to a ball at one of the big hotels. It was about 1923. I was beautifully dressed. The mayor of New York, John Hylan, comes over to me. He says: "Hello, how are you?" You know, I guess I looked like an actress or something, because I had on such a lovely dress. Jacob and Ida asked me: "How do you know Mayor Hylan?" Well, I didn't.

Another time Jacob and Ida and I went to a ball at the Astor Hotel. When I walked in, I had on a rose-colored velvet dress; it was up to my knees, with a long bodice decorated with gold beads, and a cummerbund made of pearls. You know I dressed elegantly but I never wore those mini-skirts or hot pants. There were women who dressed in such a way – you could tell they were hookers. I never dressed like that, but always elegantly and beautifully. You used to be able to tell what people did and had, almost, by the way they dressed. So, at the Astor, a fellow comes over to me. His name was Henry King. I was very attractive; I had a lovely figure, and I must have been about sixteen. Mr. King says that he would like to meet me later. My sister Ida said: "What did he say to you?" I told her. She says: "Well, you're not going to meet him later." My sister said to her husband: "What's she doing bothering a man she doesn't know?"

My brother Doc and Ida used to take me to Sam's in the Bowery. It was a nightclub with all Jewish entertainers, like vaudeville acts. I was a grown-up child, a teenager, when I went there. I think Jacob Stone and Ida also took me there sometimes; you could go. It was respectable. The entertainers were very fat and they dressed gaudy. They sang funny songs in Yiddish.

I never went to the Yiddish Theater. See, I lived uptown when I was growing up. Jacob Epstein went to the Yiddish Theater in New York and one of the people he knew from it was Molly Picon. She used to visit him when she was in London; she'd call upon him. He liked her a lot.

One of the things I did a lot of was horseback riding. I was very good at it, marvelous at it. I used to go up to resorts outside of New York City, on weekends, and I'd go riding. One place, the bridle path was through the woods and I went like Old Harry on the horse. A man was riding by and he said: "You must be a seasoned rider."

I said: "No." I think it was about the first or second ride I'd had.

He said: "Oh, you can't tell me that you're new at riding a horse, because you ride like an old timer." I'm telling you – when I think of – they go so fast. I was very lucky, you know. They gave me a spirited horse – and the trees and branches! You had to duck. Boy, I could have been killed.

We used to take vacations together after we got our lines out – all of us in the garment industry. We'd go on cruises about every two months or so, or go to places like Atlantic City. We went to Cuba a lot. I used to go to Havana on the *Morro Castle.* I remember once I told the steward on the *Morro Castle* that I was the sister of Jacob Epstein. The man was English and when he found that out – well, every night in my stateroom there'd be a bowl of crushed ice with a bowl of caviar, chopped

Plate 13: *The Tomb of Oscar Wilde*, Père Lachaise Cemetery, Paris (Jacob Epstein, stone, 1912)

Plate 16: Members of the garment industry on a vacation cruise (shipboard photograph) (seated front left: Sylvia Epstein; third from left: Hannah Troy; standing behind Hannah Troy: Al Hartman, her husband); Sylvia Epstein at Atlantic City, on the boardwalk in front of the Ritz-Carlton Hotel, c1922-23

Plate 17: Abner Epstein (later Abner Dean), c1913

Plate 18: *The Visitation*, Hirshhorn Museum and Sculpture Garden, Smithsonian Institution, Washington D.C. First cast 1926; this statue cast 1955 (Jacob Epstein, bronze)

Plate 19: 18 Hyde Park Gate, home of the Jacob Epstein family in London from 1928 to his death in 1959. The L.C.C. plaque incorrectly dates occupancy from 1929, now the home Mr. John Blackburn Gittings.

Plate 20: *New York Madonna & Child* (models: Sunita and Enver), Riverside Church, New York, N.Y. (gift of Sally Fortune Ryan) (Jacob Epstein, bronze, 1927)

Plate 21: W.H. Hudson Memorial, Rima, Hyde Park, London (Jacob Epstein, stone, 1925)

Plate 22: Fashion designers and salesmen, Sloppy Joe's Bar, Havana, Cuba, c1929-30 (left: Fannie Fox; 2nd left: Hannah Troy; centre: Sylvia Epstein)

Plate 23: S.S. Aquitania, Cruise to Nowhere, May 2-6 1931 (2nd row, fourth from left: Sylvia Epstein; 1st row, fifth from left: Vivienne Segal)

Plate 24: Alexander Press, 1930

eggs and lemons, tea, or something else to drink. Every night he'd do that.

There were wonderful hotels in Atlantic City when I went there – the *Chalfonte-Haddon*, the *Ritz-Carlton*, *The Traymore* and *The Breakers*. I stopped at *The Traymore*, and the first place I stayed at was *The Breakers*. That was a very fashionable hotel and it was the *crème de la crème* at that time. So I took a ride on the boardwalk with my girl friend. She was a bookeeper at our place. We rode in a cart with two men who were also in our business. They stood on either side of the cart. A man on the Boardwalk said I should come out. I said: "Me?"

He said:"Yes, you." So I pulled my friend along and he said: "Are you with the *Sunny Show?*" The *Sunny Show* had opened up there.*

I said: "No, I'm just a plain little girl from New York."

He said: "Well, you're sweet enough to be. What's your name?"

I said: "Sylvia Epstein. I'm from New York."

So he said: "Well, you're going to be on the front page of *The Boardwalk News*." I didn't believe it; I thought he wanted to sell photographs, but sure enough I was on the front page, along with John Barrymore and a senator and his bride. I was right there, with them all, on the front page. My brother Doc kept that picture for the longest time.

Another time I was in a place where they made beautiful evening gowns for show people. It was a wholesaler's named *Garfinkel and Siegel*, and I got a special price since I was in the business. I was buying a black-sequined evening gown to take on one of my trips. It was low-necked, skin-tight to the knees, and it had a long train. I'm wearing it in the shipboard picture with Hannah Troy. The gown is now in the historic collection of the Smithsonian Museum. So, who do I see there but Sophie Tucker. She comes up to me and says: "Hello, how are you?" I didn't know her from a hole in the wall, only I knew she was Sophie Tucker. She says: "What are you getting?".

I said: "Well, I'm going on a cruise and I need something to wear in the evening." She evidently thought I was in show business.

I had a lot of men friends, and they used to send me flowers. Orchids and gardenias. They'd put the gardenia or orchid on a band and I'd wear it on my wrist, or up here on my shoulder, or sometimes at my waist. But I never went out with artists. I went with men who were in the silver or fur business, not in my business – dresses. There was a man in the fur business who got stuck on me when I first became a model. He used to give me furs; once he gave me two fishers†. He was a widower with three children and he had a Cadillac car with a chauffeur. And he wanted to marry me. He took me to his brother's place one day. They had a big fight. The brother said to me: "You see? That's what you'll have. He killed his first wife and he'll kill you." Scared me to death. I never saw him again after that.

* * * * * *

My father gave an interview to an art magazine around 1912 in which he said that his son Jacob was a very successful and wealthy man. He infuriated Jacob, who wrote in the newspaper that his father was mistaken, that he was not at all rich. This was the truth because he and Margaret were always having a bad time with money. They always needed money. Jacob wrote Lou and asked him not to let Max Epstein seek out reporters; it was embarrassing and he felt that it could only help his enemies.

Max Epstein started going with a woman after my mother died. They were sweethearts and he wanted to get married again. He was then in his late fifties or early sixties. I don't remember the woman's name but Honey knew. She used to come and visit Honey.

Honey thought it was disgraceful. I said: "Why don't you let him get married?"

They said: "What do you know, you stinker? You don't know anything." They claimed they'd

---

*About 1925. Broadway musicals used to try out in Atlantic City before opening in New York.
†A dark brown marten fur.

have to support her, and she had a millionaire brother who said he'd support her.

Margaret Epstein was very nice to all of our family. Max went to visit her and Jacob in London and Jacob didn't pay much attention to him. The papers were full of Jacob Epstein, and my father came back with a lot of clippings. He used to sit on the subway and show them to the passengers. He'd say: "Look here, that's my son. Jacob Epstein." Once he showed them to two girls in the garment industry and they told me. Jacob, when he'd ask about his father, always said to me: "How is the old tyrant?"

Jo Davidson lived in the same neighborhood with Ida and Jacob Stone. He knew my sister very well and one day he met her on the street. He said: "Oh, Ida, how are you?" She said she was fine and she asked him about himself. Davidson told her that he was having an exhibition of his art. Ida remarked that that was nice, and he said: "You know, I'm not an Epstein." My brother Jacob never commented to me at all about Jo Davidson or his art.

CHAPTER EIGHT

Margaret, Jacob and Peggy Jean came to visit us in the United States in 1927. Jacob had returned to America for the first time in twenty-two years. Margaret had arranged portrait commissions for Jacob in New York, the two professors, John Dewey and Franz Boas, and they were working on one in Chicago. They were hoping that Jacob could do a bust of Clarence Darrow, the famous trial lawyer. Jacob was supposed to go out there to see about that while he was in America. Jacob also was to make the bronze of Paul Robeson. Jacob had met Robeson in London; he was a frequent guest in their home. Paul Robeson, so Jacob told me, had been interested in a white woman in London. She was in society and Robeson wanted to marry her. She refused, saying that it could never be, for she would be ostracized if they married. Robeson was very upset about it.

When the Epsteins came to New York they first stayed with my brother Lou. He had not yet moved out to Yonkers, but was then living at 104th Street and Central Park West. I remember the first time I saw Jacob and his family. Jacob, whom Margaret always called Jacques, was a tall, handsome man and he looked very much like the Steichen portrait made of him that year. You know, he testified for Steichen in that famous art trial they had that year over the Brancusi *Bird in Space*. The customs didn't want to let it in duty-free; they said it wasn't art. Jacob told the court that if the artist said it was art, in his opinion, it was art.

Well, Jacob wore a homburg hat then and his hair was curly and wavy, a little longer that what shows in the portrait by Steichen. Jacob always wore a homburg; he called it his lucky hat. When he was here again after World War Two he had one on with a hole in it. My brother the doctor said to him: "Jacob, aren't you ashamed to wear a hat with a hole in it? I'll give you a hat to wear."

Jacob said: "Oh, I love that hat, Irving, I love that hat." Jacob dressed nicely, but simply, in conservative clothes. He was never messy or unkempt. I don't know if he liked the portrait by Steichen, but he didn't like the one Karsh did of him. He said that Karsh said something to him; it made him upset and he *cried*. He never liked Karsh after that. Jacob said he came out of the studio, and as he went down the stairs he was crying. He didn't approve of that way of getting a picture.

Although Margaret called Jacob by a French name, we called him Jake, or Uncle Jake. My niece Marthe told me that when she went overseas as a young woman in the American Field Service in 1949, she called her uncle up in London, and arranged to see him. He was very gracious to her, and she was calling him "Uncle Jacob", when he said to her: "Marthe, would you mind calling me *Ephstein*?" That's how he pronounced it – like the German. He said "After all, you wouldn't call Donatello 'Uncle Donatello', now would you?" Kathleen Garman always called him Ephstein, too. You see, Jacob always believed in himself, and he was convinced that he was a genius. He was peculiar in that he was a very modest man about his accomplishment; but he had ego. He was an artist through and through. It's funny, but he always was afraid that someone in our family would outdo him, in his reputation. He was jealous in that way.

I met Margaret Epstein for the first time in 1927. She looked then just like a Buddha. She had hennaed hair and lovely brown eyes. She looked like my mother a lot. She didn't wear a corset or anything; everything was heavy on her. She had a heavy face with big jowls. Margaret wasn't short, but not towering either. She was heavy. . . a presence. Her feet – her feet were swollen all the time, and you couldn't see them. Her heart condition was bad. She had long skirts down to her ankles and she always dressed in dark clothes. Margaret never wore any jewelery and her clothes were not fashionable at all. She had plump hands, but her hands were not swollen as were her feet. She said to me: "Jacob does nothing but talk of you. You were a child – his little baby sister Sylvia." I can see Margaret now – fat, old, and surrounded by the many glass medicine bottles which she had with her to treat her illness.

Peggy Jean was then nine years old; she was a darling child with beautiful Titian-colored hair down to her waist. She was dressed in a very stylish green taffeta dress with long white stockings and black patent leather shoes. Peggy Jean was named after Margaret (Peggy) and the Jean was for a cat. Margaret named her for one of her cats. Yeah, for a cat. Jacob never said anything to me about the name.

Jacob and his family moved into a sublet apartment at 38 West 59th Street, where he had ample room to work on his portrait commissions. I went up to see him once while he was working on the head of Paul Robeson. My brother had large hands and he was working on the clay model, you know, with his thumbs. He'd take his big thumb and do this or that to the face. He was all smiles while he worked on it. Jacob said: "Sylvia, what do you think of the head of Robeson?"

I said: "Well, he looks very spiritual and he's looking up to God."

He said: "You're right. He's looking up to God and saying: 'What are you doing to my people?'"

I hit it on the head. I said to myself: "He's asking me a question like that? How do you like me to say that?"

While Jacob was in New York many prominent people in the theater and society would give parties in his honor, and he would decline, or decide not to go at the last moment. He told Margaret that they scrutinized him as if he were some strange creature. This disturbed him and interfered with his work.

Jacob told me that he met Chaim Weizmann through Jacob Stone while he was in New York. My brother-in-law had a specially-built Cadillac car; it was something in those days to have a Cadillac. He and Jacob went to all the places in the car and sometimes they'd take me along. They went to all the affairs, and at one of them they met Chaim Weizmann and Naftali Herz Imber, the man who wrote the *Hatikvah*, the Israeli National Anthem. Imber was then a dope fiend, you know. He was in a daze. My brother Jacob said it was such a pity that he took dope and drank. Jacob told me a lot of things.

Another person Jacob met again was Max Weber, the famous Jewish artist who lived in New York. Jacob had dinner with him in a restaurant and Max Weber would not eat lobster. He was kosher.

The Epsteins had come to America in October, 1927, and suddenly, in January, 1928, Jacob up and went back to London. He was supposed to go to Chicago to see Darrow but he didn't. He borrowed the passage money from Lou Epstein, and Ida Stone, got on the *Aquitania* and went back, leaving Margaret and Peggy Jean in New York. The borrowed money was never paid back. He went because he received word from Kathleen that if he didn't return she was going to kill herself.

Margaret and Peggy Jean had to come back after closing up the business affairs. They had brought over the Augustus John etching of Epstein and they had it in a frame in the apartment living room. They left without it and then later wrote asking for it to be sent to them, but the woman who actually sublet them the apartment took the etching and disappeared. They never got it back.

Lou Epstein was very hurt by Jacob's abrupt departure. Jacob just left, giving no explanation.

* * * * * *

Later, in July of 1928, I took a two-and-a-half-month trip abroad, visiting Jacob in London and touring the Continent. I went over on the Cunard liner *Tuscania* and returned on the French Line; I think I came back on the *France*.

The *Tuscania* sailed on July 13th at 12:01 a.m. The trip took nine days and was not too exciting. There was horse racing and shuffleboard, and no one of interest on board outside of two lovely girl friends, and Douglas and Arthur. This was the funniest foursome; of course, my friend Nan Spiro and I were their protection. You can imagine the situation, but we had more laughs than with the blooming middle-class English, and they paid for the drinks. The poor Scotchman. He was in love with the American, who was a dancing instructor, and when he got up to do a turn – well, if it wasn't for us, he would have been mobbed. There were three Schinozel boys on board. . . One Schinozel was Nan's and one was mine, but the other, he was too impossible. So you see the picking was very limited, but I made the second steward who was a doll. Of course, there was the married propositioner, but I could not be annoyed.

We arrived in London at Paddington Station on July 22nd, three in the afternoon. We finally put up in the *Park Lane,* a very ultra-fashionable hostelry equivalent to our *Ritz,* but I hoped less and inexpensive. . .

I didn't feel as fit as I should, having stayed up all night the night before to sight land. It was worth it but I was so tired that day I could hardly keep my eyes open. I wasn't going to waste any time though, so I took the phone in hand and called my illustrious brother. He answered the phone himself and recognized my voice almost immediately. He wanted me to come right over, so we, Nan and I, dressed and hopped a cab over to 18 Hyde Park Gate. The house was lovely and in a very fashionable part of London, the Kensington section off Hyde Park. It was a white house with several steps going up to a stoop. When you got to the foyer you went down into a large studio which covered the back of the house. The studio was flooded with sunlight from all sides. Trees overshadowed the open skylights. The room really would have been something to dream about if fitted up with furniture, but I knew my brother. It was just a workroom, and, no doubt, sanctuary for him.

The living room had a big piano and there was art everywhere, maquettes of work he was doing, finished pieces, other art. Art was on the tables – everywhere. When my niece Marthe visited him in 1949 and 1951, she said he had a big, carved wooden table with all kinds of things, including flowers in vases, ornaments – all cluttered. She saw two large pieces of East African art on the landing on the stairs; they were huge wooden pieces nearly six feet tall and they looked like sentinels. There were only four like them in the world, Jacob said, and he had two of them.

Upstairs there were bedrooms and they, too, were stuffed with art. Cats! Margaret had cats galore. Everywhere – cats. Margaret was seated in a chair when Nan and I came in , and alongside of her, on a chair covered with a big pillow, was a big cat. She took the cat off the chair, put it on the floor, motioned for me to sit down, and she didn't even dust off the pillow. She said: "Oh, come in. I'm so glad to see you." I had on my good clothes. I didn't say anything, and I forget now whether I sat where the cat had been, or not.

They had a Japanese butler in the house. Margaret entertained all the time. At five o'clock in the afternoon they used to have tea – every day. The most famous people in London, actresses, politicians, financiers, nobility, etc., came to tea, and a lot of the models came. Peggy Jean acted as hostess. She took me around, saying: "This is my *Ahnt* Sylvia. This is my *Ahnt* Sylvia." She was very cute.

Peggy Jean presided over the bread, jam, and butter. She was adorable with her titian hair and violet-blue eyes. She always wore a lot of green and she was dressed beautifully, in expensive children's clothes. Peggy Jean was an unusual child. You see, she met so many interesting and important people, but she had playmates. She played a lot with the children of the models. Enver, Sunita's son, was near in age. The Epsteins always encouraged her to talk and to express herself. She was not the usual precocious child of famous people.

Margaret, looking like a great Buddha, served the tea and cookies. She was always seated in an armchair at the end of the room, in the middle of the wall. Jacob would stay for a while and then disappear. He was very shy, somewhat like an adolescent boy.

When Jacob was working on his art, no one could see him for days at a stretch. Food would be brought into his studio and Margaret would return later to clear away the dishes. She would find the food untouched. During these periods he would lose a great deal of weight and become very gaunt, but when the work was finished, he was very happy. Inspiration is necessary to the life of a genius . . . They are moody and are either up in the clouds or in the depths of despair. Jacob was a man of many moods.

He loved to walk and he would often take Peggy Jean and go out and listen to the orators in Hyde Park. A lot of them made anti-Semitic remarks and this angered Jacob. He would get into heated arguments, even fights, when the speakers would shout their ugly accusations at minority groups. Peggy Jean would get very scared and would take his arm, dragging him away. Before I came, Jacob was insulted one night by another sculptor in the Café Royal. I don't know who the artist was. He had an Irish name, something like McLaughlin or Fitzgerald, and he called Epstein a dirty Jew. Jacob grabbed a wine bottle off the table and split his head open. Jacob wasn't arrested. They hushed it up. Margaret was very well-liked and she knew everybody. She had her hands full with him. Don't think it was a picnic.

Since Jacob was a Jew, this was one of the reasons why he didn't get the commissions to which he was entitled. Also, he would not be patronizing or servile. He only wanted what was rightfully his. For many years, they did not accept him in the Royal Academy. When they finally did admit him later, through other people's efforts, he resigned.

The night I arrived at 18 Hyde Park Gate I met the Indian princess Sunita and her son, Enver. She and her sister Anita were living at Jacob's. Sunita's real name was Amina Peerbhoy and her sister's name was Miriam Patel. My brother had met the two sisters at the Wembley International Exhibition of 1924. Sunita had been married to an old man who had bought her from her father. She and her sister took the child Enver and ran away from the man in the dead of night. They came to London and then they came to live at Jacob's house. She, her sister, and her child were models for Jacob. Sunita and Enver were models for *The New York Madonna and Child,* which is now at Riverside Church, New York City. Dainty? Sunita was not dainty. Her sister was dainty. Sunita, a favorite model for Epstein, was beautiful, in an Indian way. She had lovely features, but they were not small. She had beautiful, big feet. She was buxom, but very finely made, and she was a refined person.

Now Jacob was a very sexual (sensual) man, but not toward men, which was unusual at that time for artists. It's funny, but he wasn't interested in that. He was a real he-man and that runs in our family. And as far as I know, he never had an affair with Sunita, or her sister. He also did not have affairs with negro, or black women. Isn't that funny – you'd think – but he didn't. He didn't approve of homosexuality at all. He was very friendly with Gertrude Stein; he liked her and she used to come to visit him at his studio. There was a poem published in the paper about them. It went like this:

There's a wonderful family, called Stein:
There's Gert and there's Epp and there's Ein;
Gert's poems are bunk,
Epp's statues are junk,
And no one can understand Ein. *
We all had good laughs with that poem.

Jacob was very fond of Elsa Lanchester, but he couldn't stand her husband, Charles Laughton. He told me he hated the way Charles Laughton treated her. I think Laughton was a homo.

Isadora Duncan was another favorite of Epstein's. He knew her and he said that she was a very sweet woman. He liked her dancing too.

One of the people I met that first evening in 1928 was Betty Joel, the model for *La Belle Juive.* The title's right; she was an English Jewess and a very beautiful creature. * An art dealer and his wife,

*Anonymous limerick. See Willard R. Espy, *The Life and Work of Mr. Anonymous,* Hawthorne Books, Inc. New York, 1977, page 174.

*Betty Joel, daughter of Sir James Lockhart, was a famous English artist-designer of fine furniture. She had her

the Godfrey Phillips, were there also and we all went out to dinner at the Café Royal. Of course, we had everyone looking at our table as Jacob was something of a personality and habitué of the place. The *maître d'hotel* and all the people came up. Jacob was also a very big tipper. I saw many famous people there.

The next morning I had breakfast in bed and went out in the morning, at 11:30, to walk to Bond Street and, of course, we window-shopped. With all due respect to our American shops, their street was most impressive, as all the shops had different royal Coats of Arms, which were conferred by the King and Queen, Princes, and Princesses. There were three shopping centers, Bond, Regent Street, and Oxford. Cabs were cheap, so I hopped one to American Express and arranged for an afternoon bus tour of London. There was three-quarters of an hour left, so we ate lunch at an imposing restaurant, the Carlton, a French place. It had very good American prices, one pound less one-sixteenth, if you please, for lunch. It was a good thing we had limited time, or we might have had a bigger lunch.

The tour started from Trafalgar Square with its imposing statue of Charles the First. The bus took the route through the different parks, St. James, Green Park, and Hyde Park. You could see the different royal personages – Carlton House is millionaires' row. Then came Duke of Westminster and across that Duchess of Sutherland. The Prince was supposed to move from one to the other, they were saying then in London. Princess Mary had married a commoner, Viscount Lascelles*, and lived in Mayfair, a section like our Gramercy Square. Every gate in Hyde Park had some royal name such as Queen's Gate, etc.

As we were going through Hyde Park, which was tremendous, the bus driver suddenly stopped to tell about a famous sanctuary and sculptor and, of course, yours truly would tell him. Everyone got out to see as it is hidden behind bushes. It is very unusual. I would not have missed it for worlds. The Hudson Memorial, *Rima* by Jacob Epstein.

The next evening Jacob and his family took me to a Spanish restaurant and the proprietor, a Mr. Martinez, toasted us. Everything was on the house; we were his guests.

I also went sightseeing at the Royal Parish House, Windsor Castle, and Eton College, where the students came from the cream of English families. They then had a waiting list filled to 1940. The names of the prospective students were entered at birth and the list was so long that some never would get in.

When I was in London we also went to the Russian Ballet, Jacob, Margaret, Peggy Jean, and I. Margaret and Jacob were in the back of the theater discussing something with a very famous man. Peggy Jean came running down to me. She said. "*Ahnt* Sylvia, come with me. Come with me. There are some wonderful men here." She was ten years old; she was a matchmaker.

My sister-in-law Margaret thought I looked like an actress. "You remind me of Ellen Terry", she would say. "You look just like Ellen Terry." Margaret would lie down every afternoon, because of her heart condition. She had a big bed which was so low it was almost on the floor. She would talk to me while I sat with her and her main topic of conversation was Jacob Epstein. She spoke about

---

own firm, with her own factory, and she was in business with her husband, David Joel, from World War One until 1937, when she retired. The company was called *Betty Joel Ltd.* She designed fine carpets, somewhat like those designed by the Martine Workshop owned by Paul Poiret, and modern furniture adapted to contemporary British taste. The firm employed fifty craftsmen, and Betty Joel also designed furniture and sets for films. Her clients included British Airways, Lord and Lady Mountbatten, and many famous artists and businessmen. Her husband, David Joel, who opened his own business after 1937, continued the firm until after World War II. The Joel family was very influential in English finance. The family was founded by Solomon Barnato Joel, 1865-1931, whose mother was Kate Isaacs, sister of Barnato Isaacs, known as Barney Barnato. The Barnato family, to whom Max Epstein claimed relation, had extensive holdings in South Africa, particularly in diamonds.

*Princess Mary married the Earl of Harewood on February 28, 1922.

Jacob and his women. "Jacob likes women who don't have sex naturally," she told me. By that she meant he liked sophisticated sexual practices. I asked my brother the doctor if what she told me about was abnormal. He said, no, it was normal between husband and wife.

Margaret told me that Jacob had a lot of women, but that she didn't mind because none lasted long. But Kathleen – that lasted. Oh, Kathleen was a bone of contention in Margaret's life. They'd give her money to go away, and in two weeks she'd be back, and the money would be gone. Margaret did not like Kathleen at all. She would make Kathleen leave the house; the next morning Jacob would find Kathleen asleep on the doorstep. She was a problem which Margaret had not hitherto had to cope with, and so Margaret threatened Kathleen. She gave her money to go away. Margaret arranged the trip to New York in 1927 to get business for Jacob and to get rid of Kathleen for good. Margaret said she didn't want to go back home to England in 1927.

Kathleen lived in Chelsea and she posed for other artists besides Epstein. She had offers of marriage from prominent men, but she declined them all. When she posed for other artists, she annoyed them by her constant talk of Epstein. She worshipped Jacob; Margaret felt that it was not to Jacob's best interest to let this attachment go on, as he was unable to disregard Kathleen's influence. My sister-in-law told me of the letters and cablegrams from Kathleen which threatened Jacob with her suicide, and caused him to go back to London in 1927. Then Margaret told me what she did when she and Peggy Jean got back home. She said: "I shot Kathleen. Luckily it hit her in the shoulder. Kathleen lay wounded on the doorstep outside. Jacob said: 'Margaret, take her in. You can't leave her out here. Let's take her in the house. She has no place to go.' So I did. They didn't arrest me." Margaret had influence. They hushed it up.

I have never met Kathleen. While I was there in 1928, I went to an exhibition in London and I just missed seeing her. They said she had been there with the two children and just left.

Jacob wanted me to pose with Peggy Jean for a Madonna and Child while I was there in 1928. I foolishly refused to do it because I wanted to go on to the Continent. Too bad? Too bad is *right*. How I wish I had done it now.

After I had decided to go on to France, I arranged to fly the English Channel in a single-engine plane, one year after Lindbergh. Nan wouldn't fly with me because it was raining. She took the boat and met me on the other side, in Paris. Jacob said: "Oh, you're a brave girl. *You're* a *brave* girl." He carried on like something, you know. I went to Croydon and got the plane. It was some ride. They brought me up into the cockpit. We hit three air pockets going across. The weather was bad; it was thundering and lightning.

I said to myself: "Well, this is the end of me." I landed at Le Havre. When I got out of the plane they wanted to take a picture of me, posed in front of it. I was so shaken, so I said: "No, please, not after what I've been through." I got on a bus and went to Paris.

CHAPTER NINE

Nan and I went to that place, that corner place where the Americans used to go, the *Café de la Paix*, on the Rue de la Paix. We stopped at the *Brighton Hotel* on the Rue de Rivoli, near the Tivoli Gardens. After we got settled, we took a bus tour and nobody on the bus, except the tour guide, spoke English – except for two boys, two fellows. They spoke Spanish and English and they were the only ones we could talk to. They were stopping at a place in the Montmartre. So, when the tour was over, I got down out of the bus. Suddenly – you know– it was about twelve o'clock at night. I started to walk away from the bus. I was beautifully dressed. I had on a tight, green satin, Vionnet dress, criss-crossed, and I wore two silver fox furs. I had on a green felt hat, a very rakish cloche, and I was wearing snakeskin shoes with a matching purse. So four men start running after me; not after Nan, who looked like a little French girl. I looked like a German, a big blonde, and they had never seen me before.

The men were speaking French and asking me questions. I didn't understand them, or why they were running after me. I thought they wanted to hold me up. So, along comes the man from the bus, and he says to them in French: "Oh, *Americaine* girls."

"Oh, pardonnez-moi."

I said: "What do they want?"

He said: "They want to see your card, whether you have been examined by the doctor or not." They wanted to see my permit to solicit. I was a new one. They had never seen me before. The guide says to me: "No decent girl goes out at night alone. You should report in at ten."

I said: "I didn't know." He repeated that no fine girl goes out alone, so I said: "Will you take me home?"

He says: "I can't take you home. I can't afford to take you home."

So I said: "I'll pay your way. I'll pay your way home." He took me back to the Brighton Hotel in a cab.

We went to the *Folies Bergère*, at the Palace Theater. The girls wore gorgeous costumes on their heads and feet and the rest was mostly naked. They never moved, but stood still on stage. It was not trashy or lewd, since they didn't dance or do bumps and grinds. I am sitting there, talking to Nan, and an Englishman is sitting next to us. He hears me talking in English and he says: "This is very boring." The *Folies Bergère* was very long. He says: "Why don't you ladies come with me and I will show you Paris?" I said no, that I wanted to hear the singing. I had gone there because I wanted to hear a certain Spanish girl sing *Who Will Buy My Violets?*

The man said: "Well, she's from my town – Barcelona. She was a street girl, for a quarter. I'll take you places where you can see. . . " He was in the cork business. Champagne corks. His father manufactured them in London. So, after the singer, we went with him and he took us to the *Moulin Rouge* first. Mistinguette was there, and he bought champagne galore. He didn't finish the bottle – he was opening another. We'd take one drink and he'd open another bottle. So I passed the open bottles around to the entertainers and chorus girls there and they were all drinking with us.

Then he took us to a place at 32 rue Blondel. You'd go in and they'd have a stage setting. They had a hermaphrodite and the woman he or she was living with. . . married to. . . having an affair with. They'd show the testicles and the vagina. She had one of each and she, he, was living with this girl. They had sex on stage. Embarrassed? No, I didn't know what I was seeing. I knew a hermaphrodite. I had heard of them. Hermaphrodites had two things – a penis and a vagina. But – there were other people there. I didn't know what they were doing. She, he, wore her hair short. She was both a man and a woman. So what the hell? She had a little penis. What could she do to that woman? Not much.

So what was that man doing taking us there? I don't know. I used to meet a lot of people on my trips, but I always travelled with friends, never alone. He wanted to take me to Saint Cloud the next day, and I was going to go, but, luckily, he ran out of money, because he was spending so much money. So he says to Nan: "You'll have to give me some money until I see you tomorrow." I give my friend a kick under the table. *She* was going to give him money. The next morning he calls on the phone and he says: "I was called back to London, a hurried call, and I have to go back." Wasn't that smart ? I don't know whether he was a scoundrel or not. He wasn't a gigolo, though. If she gave him fifty dollars –if I gave him fifty dollars – I'd be out fifty dollars. A nice man, though.

Then we took a tour to go to Vienna. We went to Berlin – I've got pictures of Berlin, on the bus, on the main street, the Kurfürstendam, and we stopped at the *Adlon*. We went to Innsbruck. It took sixteen hours, and I had about $250 cash in my pocketbook. You know, you stop in those foreign train compartments. I thought if I'd fall asleep someone would rob me. So, I said: "Where is the next stop?" Oh, they had sleepers there, *Schalfwagen.* You know, I speak a little German, so I said: "Nan, let's go and look for a *Schalfwagen."* We went through second class, third class, and they're sleeping on the floor. They're *sleeping* on the *floor.* We get to the *Schalfwagen* and there's the man of the *Schalfwagen,* and I said, ah, I said in German, does he have a *Schlafwagen* for us to go to Vienna?

He says: "Nein."

So, with that, I had to use the toilet very badly, and I was afraid to use the toilets where we were. I see *Damenzimmern.* So – *Damenzimmern* – I go in and the window was open. I closed the window and a pane of glass falls out. I used the toilet and I go back. Suddenly the man from the *Schalfwagen* is knocking on the window of my compartment. I said: "Nan, he's got a *Schalfwagen* for us."

She goes out and comes back and says: "He doesn't want me. He wants you."

I go out and ask him what he wants. He says: "I – *Du hast das Fenster gebrochen. Du musst elf Schilling bezahlen!"* That means eleven shillings. It's about two and a half dollars in Viennese money. Because I broke the window in the toilet, he says, see?

So I said: *"Nicht ich, ich bin Amerikaner, ich bezahlen nicht."* I said: "I'm an American, but I don't pay."

So he says: *"Oh, die Polizei!"* He's going to get the police. So the next stop was Innsbruck, and, in the meantime, there were two other girls in our compartment and they were going to stop at the *Ritz* in Innsbruck. They had reservations. Innsbruck is only about two blocks long. Oh, it's a beautiful place. So when I got there, the man from the *Schlafwagen* spots me. He says: *"Ach, das ist das Mädchen was said mein hals schneiden."* He said that I had said that I was going to cut his throat, when he started to make me pay, but what I'd really said was that when the chicken went to the axe, then I'd pay him; he'd get the two and a half dollars from me. He was saying: *"Guck, ich aus die Mädchen that das ein hals schneiden."* He kept saying that I was the girl who was going to cut his throat. He said that I had to pay for the window. He runs across the track and goes to get the police – *"Oh, Die Polizei –."*

Along comes the policeman with a big, long cape and a hat with a feather floating down. The man from the *Schlafwagen* says: *"Das ist die Madchen that –."* They had those wheelbarrow carts to carry the luggage in, and while they're talking, the porter of one says to me:

"Where are you going to stop?"

I says: "The *Ritz.*" I have no reservation and the music festival is on. There are no rooms, so the luggage man goes from one hotel to another. I get to one hotel and there's a man there who speaks

English. He says he has been to Washington and stopped at the *Raleigh*. I had stopped at the *Raleigh*. I said that I was an American girl and that I hadn't got a reservation. He said that he didn't have a reservation for me either, but that he would allow me to sleep in the salon. They had two little chairs, two settees. For Nan it was all right, but for me it wasn't. The policeman had said that he was going to decide the next morning whether or not I had to pay for the window, so I said: "I'm going to get on the first train that goes out in the morning. " The hotel man told me that the first one was at six, so he wakes me for six. Somebody had checked out of a room, and we went up and used it to wash up, and then had our breakfast. I gave the man, whose name was August, a dollar apiece from Nan and me. He had been very nice to us. We were on that six o'clock train and we got out of there.

We also went through Prague, and I remember stopping off in the station on the way to Vienna, to get a drink of water at one of those kiosks. The girl wanted to charge me five cents for a glass of water. There was a man there, a tall, handsome fellow. His name was Egon Bic, from Vienna. He heard the girl say five cents, and he said to her: "Give her that water and no five cents. I never heard of that." Egon Bic was visiting an Englishman in Vienna, a man named Weinstein originally; he had changed it to Winston. He was a very attractive man, this man Winston, and he was from London. He was married to an American girl, and my friend, Fannie Fox, knew him. When she found out I was going to Vienna, Fannie told me to call him up. So I did, and I got his wife, who was very jealous of him. She's asking me how did I know him – I told her I heard of him through Fannie Fox, but this woman wants to know if I'm having a affair with him, or what. His name was Bert Weinstein and he was head of a big shoe firm in London. They were very rich. I think his first wife died, and he later married a *shiksa*. Bert even came to see me in the United States after I had married.

We travelled around in Europe, saw the sights, and I did a lot of shopping for myself in the department stores, buying shoes, and things, and coming home to America in October, 1928.

CHAPTER TEN

I stayed with Wonder Dress for many years. I was both saleswoman and designer. The garment district was anywhere from 40th Street down to 35th Street, between Broadway over to Eighth Avenue. Most of the garment center's buildings were on Broadway and Seventh Avenue. The Wonder Dress Company moved up to 500 Seventh Avenue, and that was a swanky building. I went along and the owner of the company didn't want to pay me the money I was making. I was making very good money, and he said: "A girl should make so much money?"

So I left, and I worked for another firm. I brought in big accounts like Lerner's. They'd give me a thousand of a number for an order; sometimes they'd pick two or three numbers and I'd come back with an order for 3,000 dresses. My boss would say: "A girl should bring back such business?" I told Ida that I wanted to leave. Ida was shocked.

She said: "You're crazy to leave. Where will you get a job and make the money you're making?"

I said: "Well, I'm worth more." And that's how I got the name for my own dress company, *The Worthmore Dress Company.* A girl who was a saleswoman was very friendly with me, and she said:

"Sylvia, would you like to go into business? I know my old boss went out of business and he's looking to go into business again."

I said: "Yes, I'll go into business." I had saved money from my salary and I cashed in an insurance policy for over five thousand dollars. I had to put up $8,300 for my share of capital. I went into business with two men. One of them was named Sonny Abrams; that's the one I remained in business with, for I got rid of the other man later. He was buying things from his brother and getting a rake-off. I paid him out and lost six thousand dollars there. After that Sonny Abrams was a watch dog, and I did most of the designing, buying, and selling. Oh, I did everything. I had a natural flair for it, and I knew how to draw and paint. Never took a lesson in my life. I was mainly self-taught, like my brother Jacob. I had a French girl in the company; she could sketch. I had patternmakers in my firm, for I was above making patterns. I'd go to the stores, or see a Paris original, and come back with an idea. I'd tell it to the French girl and she'd sketch it. I didn't drape much. Sometimes I'd go over to the model, put a bow on, or say: "Put piping there", or adjust it somewhat. Other times I'd buy a dress and bring it down in price. The change would be in the material, the quality, and the adjustment of design. The workmanship would remain the same; it was very good. I used good materials though, and my price range was wholesale $10.75 to $16.75, retail $16.75 to $29.95. We made only misses clothes and we did daytime and streetwear only.

Worthmore was at 525 Seventh Avenue. We had a loft, and I bought fabrics; everything was wholesale. The wholesalers of materials were all along Broadway and they'd bring in their samples. I'd look at materials; make up a design with the French girl. I did it all — I made the bows on my outfits, for I made fancy bows. I made hats by hand. I'd make daytime suits, outfits with smart coats and matching hats.

We had thirty-six girls at the Singer machines, and five more seamstresses at machines in the room where I'd make my models up. I had two or three cutters, three or four presses, and about ten girls who were finishers. There were one or two patternmakers; the patternmakers made good money, around $200 a week. A good cutter and a good presser made $150 a week. I also employed two or three girls as models, and three men as salesmen, although I did most of the selling. Detail work was sent out, and we used a lot of embroidery, especially the Schiffli embroidery. All in all, we

Plate 25: Sylvia & Al Press with Sylvia's Buick, on honeymoon at Roscoe, N.Y., June 1936; Leda & Ian Hornstein, c1944

Plate 26: *Lucifer*, By Courtesy Birmingham Museums & Art Gallery, England (Jacob Epstein, gold-patinaed bronze, 1944)

Plate 27: Sir Jacob Epstein, Hyde Park Gate, 1949; Jackie, Sir Jacob & Marthe Epstein, 1949

Plate 28: *The Liverpool Giant*, Lewis's Dept. Store, Liverpool, England (Jacob Epstein, bronze 1954)

Plate 29: Three bas-reliefs: *Children Playing*, Lewis's Dept. Store, Liverpool, England (Jacob Epstein, concrete, 1954)

Plate 30: Central bas-relief from *Children Playing* (Annabel Freud & Frisky)

Plate 31: Lucien Freud holding Annabel Freud, 1949

Plate 32: *Social Consciousness*, Fairmount Park Art Association, Philadelphia, Pa (Jacob Epstein, bronze, 1954)

Plate 33: Shipboard photograph: Chana Solomon & Sir Jacob Epstein, 1954; Long Beach, N.Y.:
Sir Jacob Epstein, Sylvia Press Epstein, Dr Irving Epstein, 1954

Plate 34: *Ecce Homo*, St Michael's Cathedral, Coventry, England (Jacob Epstein, stone, 1935)

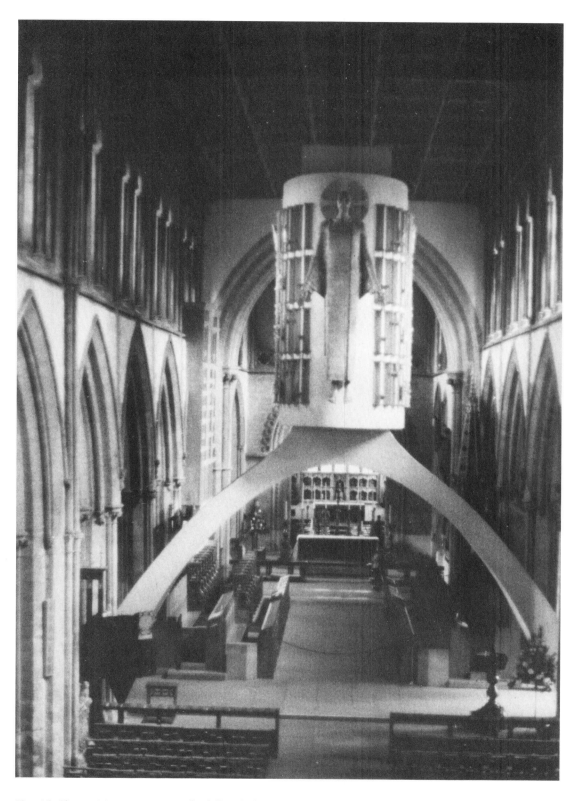

Plate 35: *Christ in Majesty (Majestas)*, Llandaff Cathedral, Cardiff, Wales (Jacob Epstein, aluminium, 1955), By Permission of the Dean and Chapter of Llandaff Cathedral, Cardiff, Wales

Plate 36: *Youth Advancing*, Manchester City Art Galleries, Manchester, England and London Art Service, Ltd. (Jacob Epstein, bronze, 1949)

employed about fifty or sixty people at Worthmore.

The shop was organised. Our union was The International Ladies Garment Workers Union. We didn't have much labor trouble, except with one man. It was in 1930, when I started the company. I had to get rid of my foreman. He was Jewish and he used to stink up the place with herring. He said to me: "I'll break you. I'll put you out of business."

I said: "You'll never put me out of business." So I wanted to fire him and I had to have the o.k. from the union. I was very friendly with one of the union men. He said: "It'll cost you $250, Miss Epstein." I paid it, and I got rid of the foreman. He was just making trouble for me.

I sold the dresses only in the United States, but, see, I'd been a model and a saleswoman, and I knew a lot of people. I sold Lord & Taylor, Franklin Simon, Saks Fifth Avenue, McCreery's, Altman's — I sold every good store. I also sold to The May Company in California, and to a big store down in Miami. I often sold my clothes to Lazarus Brothers; they had the AMC chain, but I never sold to Sears & Roebuck, for they were too cheap. I'd do my own selling, going to big places like Kirby, Black & Fisher or Perry Schwab. As I said, I'd get called in and the salesmen would get so jealous. You know, a lot of the buyers and operators in the industry were women. They were a very big factor in the development of the industry. Women could go as far as they wanted in it, if they were good enough, but the men resented it. It is also very important to be well liked in the business, and I was well liked. I was friendly and I had a lot of friends and a nice reputation. I'd also advertise my clothes; if you helped pay the expenses, the stores would advertise your line, but you had to pay extra for credit for your line, and I never did that. We'd advertise the designs in the Sunday edition of *The New York Times* — newspapers like that — but we didn't advertise in *Vogue* or *Harper's Bazaar*, as that was too expensive.

Well, I made good money, for in a good year, having my own factory and low overhead and taxes, I'd gross a half million, $600,000. Of course, there was my partner; he got half, after expenses. I'd give myself a bonus all the time, such as a car or a new fur coat. I bought my first car in 1932. I loved furs and I bought myself the white ermine coat, full length to the floor, which you can see in my picture at Sloppy Joe's Bar in Havana. In a good year, around 1932, I made $15,000 to $20,000.

I had a lot of men friends but I was not married and continued to live at Ida's. Ida was very religious and went to a very swanky temple, where Rabbi Herbert Goldstein was head, but I was not religiously inclined. Chana and Ida were religious, but Jacob, Harold and I were not. I observed the religious holidays and, when my sister insisted, I went to the temple. I also gave to the temple where Ida went.

Well, I worked hard. I got to work very early in the morning, 8:30 a.m. I would go out to see buyers between 8:30 and 9:30, and then I'd go to Schrafft's on Broadway, to have coffee. All the people in the trade would be there and we'd talk shop. I used to see Lucille Ball in Schrafft's every day. She was a model in the garment center then, and she'd always be there with a man whose family I knew. They were from the same town — Augustów — that my family was from. He was in ready-to-wear. Lucille Ball was a nice-looking girl and she was well-dressed, not flashy, but you could tell she was a model by the way she dressed.

After 10:30 I'd go back to my place because the buyers would start coming in. Lunch was at one o'clock, and if I had an appointment with a buyer, we'd go up to the Savoy-Plaza, and I'd take him to lunch. All my buyers never paid for lunch if I was around. Of course, I'd take it off my expenses. If I didn't have a date for lunch, I'd go to Schrafft's for about a half-hour. It was then back to the loft to look at fabrics, which would be brought in in the afternoon, and I'd work with the five girls at the machines in the model room, and tell them what I wanted. My day ended at six, six thirty, and if I didn't have a date with a buyer, I'd go home to dinner at Ida's. We worked Monday through Friday, with a half-day on Saturday. So, you can see why we always took a two or three week vacation every two months, when we got out our lines.

Men – I had dates always. I would go with them; I would like them, and then I'd get tired of them. I'd turn off of them. Even my husband later. I had a good salary; I bought what I wanted, and I went to the swankiest places. I used to go with men who were brokers, and I had my nose up in the air. I thought I was the cat's meow, and the men – they just never lived up to my expectations. I only liked one man, a drummer. He was in the silverware business, Cohn-Rosenberger. I got, through his brother, silverware and things. He gave me real pearls, and even Leah got things from him. I used to have charms that dangled – you put coins in them – made of sterling silver – from him. Oh, he was – he used to make about $250 a week, in those days a lot of money. He wanted to marry me. My sister Ida didn't want him to marry me. She didn't like him because he was a little shorter than me. She said: "You're going to marry a little shrimp like that?" Ida liked good-looking men.

He brought a ring around, about a carat diamond. He says to me: "I suppose if you show that to your sister, she'll laugh at it?"

I said: "You said it."

He said: "Well, that puts you – will you marry me and go to Chicago?" Chicago was his route. I said, no, that I didn't want to leave New York. So he went to Chicago but he used to write me letters. He met a girl that lived in Minneapolis and he married her. So he wrote me that he got married being as I thought that no one was good enough for me. I cried. I *cried,* and I used to meet him on 34th Street after he was married. He'd come in from Chicago and I would meet him. He had two children and he'd take out the pictures. I wasn't married.

He'd say: "You see? They could have been yours. But you think you're Lord Kakeyak. No one's good enough for you." Later he became a millionaire. He's dead now. Well, you see, my family didn't like him and I was making good money in New York. Chicago was a long way away. We had relatives there. My cousin Jane of Chicago was a reporter on the *Telegraph.* She wrote up the movies, and she went with a very fast crowd. She knew Fatty Arbuckle and that girl, Virginia Rappe. She said Virginia Rappe was a beautiful girl, but that it was a very fast bunch. She didn't know the facts about the scandal. Anybody who went with my cousin Jane was fast though, because she was. She had a bad reputation. Her father was my father's brother, the one who met my father at Castle Garden.

Jane of Chicago was really named Jennie Epstein, but we called her Jane because she married a Gentile, Bill Cressy. He was a big, handsome man, and he was the insurance man for all the movie actors and actresses of that time. He was very successful. Jane's father disowned her because she married a *goy.* Cressy was very good to my cousin. She came to see us with him, and she had a lovely ring with three big diamonds in it. Cressy died and Jane married again, to an American-Portuguese Jew – by the name of Rinaldo. She said later that she was sorry she married him because he was not physically what Cressy had been. Jane was a short, fat girl, but she was sexy. She liked sex. Cressy was a very handsome man and sexy.

We also had other relatives in the Midwest. Their name was Goldberg and they were my mother's brother's family. One of their sons was Leonard Gilbert – he changed the name. He went to West Point and he graduated, but later he got ill with some disease and wasn't able to continue his army career. He lived in Cleveland, I believe.

There was a Gentile who wanted to marry me. My family was against it. I wouldn't go with him unless I took all my friends along. He was an importer and he was Hungarian. His name was Stefan. He had studied for the opera, and he was anti-Semitic. I said to him: "What do you want with me? I'm a Jewess."

He said: "Oh, you don't look Jewish. You don't act Jewish." I didn't look Jewish.

Ida used to say to me: "You're going to get a bullet one of these days. You're fooling him and he wants to marry you." He used to bring me presents every Friday night – flowers and a gift. Once he brought me a beautiful, antique, Venetian glass decanter. I found out he was stealing from the stock.

I told him that I had too a good reputation as a businesswoman and came from too distinguished a family to accept any more such presents.

Another man I went around with was Hattie Carnegie's brother. He was a nice man and I went with him because he was her brother. Hattie Carnegie – my God in Heaven, that was something. She was a very big designer. She did everything – hats, clothes, jewelery. She was a very attractive woman, too. You see, being a model and all, I made a good appearance and I was a good dancer. He liked to take me out. He was an only brother and he was a salesman for Hattie Carnegie. I think she also had a sister in the suit business. Her brother took me to one place; it was a wholesaler's, and I bought gold pins shaped like chickens, with rubies for eyes. I got a checked dress from Hattie Carnegie through him. He'd tell me about his sister and he wanted me to meet her, but I never did get to know her.

I knew the hat designers in New York – Irene, Lily Daché, and John-Fredericks*, which later became Mr. John. I'd have hats made. I got hats from Lily Daché. She was a very talkative woman, and full of life. She was no beauty, but she was not homely, quite attractive, in fact. She was very nice to me because we were all in the dress business. I used to meet people and I brought them to her, and to John-Fredericks also. Lily Daché gave me a special price, being in the business.

I used to go to John-Fredericks and I knew both of them very well. Mr. John's real name was Hansi Harburger and he was born in Vienna. In 1929 he became partners with Frederick Wirst; the firm had their combined names. Fred managed the business end and John was the designer. He was a wonderful designer. I knew them both so well; we were good friends. I used to go to their apartment on Madison Avenue and 72nd Street. I'd bring people to them, too, and they'd give me special prices. I just bought their hats; I picked what I wanted, but never designed with any of the designers to make up my hats. I remember John making a hat for me of felt. It was turned up in front and he had made little bows of different colors on it. They snapped on and I could change the colors of the bows all the time. I could match the hat up with my outfits. Fred was very fond of me. Their hats were very expensive – fifty, sixty, even a hundred dollars apiece, but I'd get them for fifteen, sixteen dollars. I'd say: "I don't want to spend that (fifty – or whatever), Fred. I can't afford it."

He'd say "Don't worry, Sylvia. We'll fix up the price." They sold to everybody – movie stars, society women, theater people. That hat firm was something. They were even in the newsreels all the time.

John used to play funny tricks on me, or any other customer he was friendly with. He'd bring over a hat. You know, a lot of his customers were society women. He had a thing shaped like a curd. It was an artificial curd and he'd put it in the hat. He'd say: "She's going to try this on." We'd all laugh. It was the kind of thing he always did. He was full of hell.

They were both very handsome men. Fred was tall and John was short. I met Fred first. I went on a trip with him to the Panama Canal and we went through the locks. I went with Fred and we took a hydroplane over them. He was scared; he was holding my hand. He said: "Oh, Sylvia, I'm nervous."

I said: "Don't be nervous. Nothing will happen to you."

We got off the plane and we went to Colon. Colon was a pretty fast city. It had all brothels. The prostitutes stood outside and they'd call the sailors, or whoever, in. They even called me in. "Ohhhh. Exhibition. *Exhibition*", like in French, you know. They are going to show me an exhibit.

So I said: "What the hell do they want?"

The men with me said: "Don't you know what she wants? They don't care who they take."

So there was one Jewish girl there, from Poland, and I spoke to her. She spoke Yiddish and I understand it, you see. She told me that she had been disowned by her parents because she got mixed up this way. She said: "But, I don't. . . You know, I never let any of them touch my breasts."

*Also known as John Frederics.

I'll never forget her saying that. I said: "Why?"

She said: "You get flabby if they touch your breasts. And I don't want my breasts to get flabby."

Fred made me a hat down in Panama. He got a Panama straw and he draped it on my head. Then he pinned it and said to me: "Now, you stitch it where I've pinned it." I did and I wore it. I had paid fifty cents for the straw hat. Everyone said: "Where did you get that hat?" It was beautiful.

Fred said: "Now, don't ever tell that I did this – that I'm from Mr. John."

John and Fred had a falling out in 1948 and Fred left the business. John got another partner, Peter Brandon, and opened up again in 1948 as Mr. John. Fred and John split up because Fred wanted to marry a banker's daughter. He had met the girl on a boat trip. The people were Jewish and the girl was all of eighteen years old. Fred was in his thirties then. So when the people came back, they told one of their friends that their daughter was going to be engaged to Fred of John-Fredericks. Now, these people were very dear friends of the bank, and they said: "What, are you crazy? Don't you know he's a queer?" So they broke it off.

Fred confided in me a lot. He said: "How do you like that, Sylvia? They dropped me like a hot potato."

I said: "Well, you can't blame them, Fred." I mean, what was in it for her? I don't know if he was bi-sexual, or what.

Another famous designer I used to buy from was Ben Zuckerman. He made beautiful coats and suits and I got mine there wholesale. Ben Zuckerman lived in a very exclusive, swanky apartment house. He had the penthouse and his mother lived with him. She wouldn't stay up there, but every day she would come downstairs with her chair, and go outside, to sit in front of the apartment house. The management overlooked it for a while, but then the doorman said: "Mr. Zuckerman, your mother can *not* sit outside this door. We cannot allow this. The landlord does not want it."

Mr. Zuckerman said: "Well, you see, my mother doesn't want to sit up on the roof. She can't see anybody there. She wants to see people." Oh, how we laughed about that. She was just a simple, plain woman from the Lower East Side.

There was another joke we told about the garment industry. I don't know if it was true or not, but it seems that there was this woman who had been in the dress business and her husband had really made it big in the stock market. They moved out to the suburbs to a beautiful, fancy house and she wanted to entertain all her old friends in New York. So she invited them for the evening, and, at the last minute, she is checking her bathrooms, and she sees that she hasn't any toilet paper. So, it's too late to go to the store, and she runs around and she finds her old patterns. She tears them up and sticks them in the toilet paper holder. The people come and they are admiring everything. The next day the two women guests meet in New York and they discuss the newly-rich friend. One woman says: "Such a beautiful house I've never seen."

The other one says: "You're right, and did you see the chandelier? So beautiful."

The first woman says: "Right. And did you see the toilet? I've never seen such wealth. She even had toilet paper marked front and back."

CHAPTER ELEVEN

We had a lot of fun in the garment industry. Every Saturday night we used to have parties. Now we don't for the men are all dead. I'd wear my black-sequined gown with a big black straw hat. I'd stick a rose on top of it and one under my ear. I had a long, black chiffon handkerchief attached to my little finger. I'd get up and dance and sing. I'd make up all kinds of songs in pretend French. I didn't know what I was saying. One man was a very good piano player – it was such fun.

A lot of the men in the industry were homosexuals. It was commonplace and accepted. I knew a lot of homosexual designers – it was not hidden. If I went on a trip or a cruise, they'd often be there with their friends in the ready-to-wear because they used to use their silks. If the men weren't homosexual, sometimes they'd take up with men who'd make them homosexual. It was a way of climbing for a man who was a nothing. Some of the salesmen and designers were kept by very big male designers. They'd learn the business that way sometimes.

There used to be big homosexual balls held at 107th Street, Lexington, and Park. Designers – everybody went to the drag balls, and the whole gang got together from the industry, even the men and their wives. One fellow I knew from the industry, a dress designer, went all the time. He had a millionaire keeping him. There were a lot of rich Japanese men at those balls. Everybody would dance, and the men would dance together. They had entertainment. It was hired for the balls and consisted mainly of professional transvestites. They were not from the garment industry. My friend Eva was going with the man who became her first husband later. His name was Henry Walden. He was a dentist and also an early bird – an aviator whose name is in the Smithsonian. He was a very handsome man. A Japanese man came up and asked him to dance. Eva's fiancé wasn't a fag, but she got scared. She said: "Oh, my God, he's acting like a fag. I'm afraid to marry him."

Some women didn't care if the men were homos. I knew one couple down south – she was an older woman, a retired actress. Her husband was a very handsome young man and he was homosexual. He used to do all the buying for his wife's shop, and I sold to them. He said: "My wife was a famous actress." You see, she had gotten old and opened up a dress shop down south. He found out I was Jacob Epstein's sister and he said: "I must bring my wife up here to meet you." I didn't say anything. I knew he was a homo; he was gorgeous-looking, but he was very feminine. He says to me: "You know, I don't take up with everybody." He brought his wife to meet me and I became very friendly with both of them. He was a companion to this woman, you see.

One of the cruises I went on was the first Cunard *Cruise to Nowhere.* It was from May 2nd to 6th 1931. We went out from New York on a Saturday, on the *Aquitania.* We cruised down the Gulf Stream to Bermuda and came back on the following Tuesday. It cost very little, from fifty dollars to $150 for the four days. We were on it only for pleasure, and the first and second class quarters were all open to us. There were all kinds of recreation – swimming, dancing, lectures, bridge tournaments, movies, and deck sports. We drank a lot of cocktails, too; some people thought that was the main reason for these cruises, since we were still in Prohibition. There were six hundred people on board. I had my picture taken on the ship, and there were very interesting people on the trip. One of them was Vivienne Segal, the actress. You can see her in the picture. Another one was William Randolph Hearst, Jr. He was then married to his first wife; she was in show business and I don't think his family approved of it. We had dancing every evening and everyone wore beautiful evening clothes.

William Randolph Hearst, Jr., came up and asked me to dance with him, and I did. What the hell can you do on a Cruise to Nowhere? Entertain yourself. We broke the speed record coming back to New York, making the trip back in twenty-nine hours and twenty-five minutes.

Ida Stone lived in an apartment house right next to William Randolph Hearst on Riverside Drive. He and his family lived at 137 Riverside Drive and 86th Street. We lived in the next house at 86th Street; the Hearsts had the corner house. I used to see the old man coming home – square-shouldered and tall. He had a high-pitched voice. I used to see the twin boys playing in the street.* The Hearsts owned the large apartment house on Riverside Drive and they occupied the top three floors. The top floor was a ballroom. I never went to their house, but I remember when they entertained Admiral Byrd when he came back from the North Pole.** They had a doorman for the house and they put out the red carpet. I went down to listen to all the names of the guests; they called them out as they entered. I heard them call out the family of Fells. And Admiral Byrd came in all his regalia. I stood there watching him go up. You know, I was very young at the time.

I met Mrs. Hearst some years later when she came to the dress business with a famous designer whose name I can't now remember. Mrs. Hearst was lovely – a very nice woman. Of course, when I lived next door to them – this was before William Randolph Hearst met Marion Davies and moved to the Coast. My cousin, Jane of Chicago, was very friendly with Marion Davies, and she was also very friendly with her older sister, René. Marion Davies was a very comely girl, very nice, but she was not considered at all trampy. I also never heard that she was considered to be funny – a comedienne. She had absolutely no ability as an actress. She was a very simple girl before they glamorized her as The Blonde. She met Hearst, and, of course, she wanted to get somewhere and so William Randolph Hearst was the proper man to put her there.

Besides men, I had a lot of women friends. They liked me, mainly because I could drive a car, I think. Fannie Fox used to call me every Sunday morning – early, about six. The phone would ring and Ida would say: "That's that Fannie Fox calling you." Fannie called I should put her first on my list to go somewhere, for every Sunday we'd go out in my car and I'd take my girl friends along.

Then I met Al, my husband, and everything started to go bad after that. Al's name was Alexander Press and he was born on the Lower East Side, on Henry Street, near the Henry Street Settlement. His birth date was August 3, 1900. Al didn't know one word of Yiddish. His family later moved up to the Bronx, and, of course, we people who lived in Manhattan turned our noses up at people who lived in the Bronx.

Al's father was named John Press and he made ladies' beaded bags. Mr. Press changed his name from Abe to John when he went into the handbag business because the company, Beaman's, said they couldn't have the name Abe. Al's father was a friend of Adolph Zukor's. They both came from Russia, I think, and they knew each other on the Lower East Side. Zukor took Al into his *Famous Players-Paramount Pictures* Company. They wanted Al in the business end and he did that, but Al also played in their movies when he was a young man of eighteen or nineteen. He was a supporting actor. Al was very good-looking and he played with women who were famous headliners. One famous actress was stuck on him. I can't now remember their names or the movies they played in, as it happened before I met Al. We've looked and looked, but we haven't been able to find any record of Al in the movies at all. He played under his name, Alexander Press, and he also used the name Al Preston. Al never went to Hollywood to work. He made movies in Westchester County, New York, and Fort Lee, New Jersey. He was extremely handsome and he dressed beautifully. This was always very important to Al; he was proud of me because I dressed so well. Al was a real ladies' man, with

---

*The Hearst's had five sons: George, William Randolph, Jr., John Randolph Apperson, and his twin, Elbert Wilson, who changed his name to David Witner. See Davies, Marion, *The Times We Had, Life with William Randolph Hearst*, Bobbs Merrill, Indianapolis, 1975, for material on the Hearst Family.
**1926 or 1929.

good manners and charm. Women were crazy about him.

Al was very friendly with all the movie people and he was friendly with people in The Mob. The Mob liked Al; he never had to pay protection when he went into business. I never had anything to do with the Mob. We both knew William Fox of Fox Film Corporation, and Al went with his daughter for a while. Al went with a lot of movie women. He knew Esther Ralston and Alice Brady. He also knew Fannie Brice. He used to be invited to Fannie Brice's house at Huntington, Long Island, because he went out with Fannie's sister. Al never commented about his girls. I do know that he knew Ruth Chatterton, although he never played in the movies with her. He was crazy about Ruth Chatterton's niece, whom he met on a trip. She was a beautiful young girl, and I think he was in love with her, but something happened; what I don't know.

After Al left the movies, he worked in the garment center as a coat salesman. He had quite a few houses; this was before he met me. Al pursued me intensely when we met. I met him through Ralph Krause, who was going with a very pretty girl. She was a hat model. Ralph used to say to Al: "I'd invite you along if you'd go with someone decent. You go with tramps all the time. I know a decent girl and I'm going to introduce her to you; otherwise you can't go with us." That girl was me. Al took me to The Tavern on the Green in Central Park and he proposed one week later.

My sister Ida said she didn't want me to be an old maid. I had a very lucrative business and I just didn't want to get married. Ida was afraid I'd get mixed up with some man and I wouldn't get married. She liked Al because he was handsome and charming. After I got engaged, I wanted to break it off, but she wouldn't let me. She was so persistent; it was something terrible. I just didn't want to marry him. We were married on June 3, 1936, and we went up to Roscoe, New York, to Tanana Lake House, for our honeymoon. On our honeymoon I cried a lot. Oh, I was sorry I married him. What did I want in a man? I never wanted a man like my brother Jacob. As far as I was concerned, he was a doll, but he was no man any woman should have married. I liked a man who was good-looking – that I got. I also wanted a man with a lot of money – that I didn't get. I found out after we were married that neither Al nor any other in his family was working. The man who ran the resort at Tanana Lake House tried to interest me in investing in resort cottages up there, but I was afraid to, as I didn't know how the marriage would work out. I put my husband in the dress business. He opened up an evening dress company, but evening dresses are expensive. Al was no manager and he was not liked in the garment industry.

Ida was a wonderful woman, like a mother to me, but she was too much that way. If I knew then what I know now, I would have never listened to Ida. I think I would have married the drummer and gone to Chicago.

After we got back from our honeymoon, we moved into my mother-in-law's apartment on West 113th Street. In August I got a letter from Margaret Epstein. She and Jacob are sending me an Epstein watercolor of roses for a wedding present, and they want to send Peggy Jean to me. Peggy Jean was running around, night-clubbing, and she was going to all the colored clubs. Margaret was worried that she would get mixed up with one of the men there.

LETTER FROM MARGARET EPSTEIN TO SYLVIA EPSTEIN PRESS

[Dated] 6 August 1936

18 Hyde Park Gate
SW7

[TOP OF PAGE BEFORE SALUTATION]

[LEFT]

This is a very private letter. Burn it when you've read it. Letters can cause mischief often by accident.

[RIGHT]

I should like to typewrite this scrawl but you'll be able to read some of it.

[ALONG LEFT SIDE MARGIN]

P.S. Time is short. Perhaps she can do it. She can get a few rags together and the fare & a little over which she must give you to keep for her & plan at least a holiday for her.

At the moment we are in the hands of money lenders.

Dear Sylvia, This is just in case we get Peggy-Jean on board to you in 10 days or so I was thinking of your kind invitation to Peggy Jean for a visit.

She might benefit by it immensely just at the moment I think.

She has celebrated her last governess's disappearance by dancing all night and sleeping all day for quite a spell — too long a spell. There are too many night clubs here of not too white a record. You don't quite have what I mean in New York. Not mixed up so much.

Perhaps it could be found out what

[SECOND PAGE]

would be charged at the arts students League her father's old school for her for a term of drawing & painting. Also for a music term. She has never really worked at these although she has decided vocation

[ALONG LEFT MARGIN]

She just would not apply herself to drudgery which is what makes the genius given the bent

[SECOND PAGE CONTINUED]

We are because of what you know of of [sic] our secret life's complication always on the verge of bankruptcy but I could scrape something together for her school fees and pocket money.

You & I could keep an a/c & what you spent I could refund when I could. Our income is so irregular & so fantastically spent you would get the astonishment of your life if you had a glance at it. I've been better in health since my baby son was born 2 years ago next month. *

[THIRD PAGE]

Some day Peggy-Jean should get married
of course. Perhaps some nice Doctor Jewish-Scotch or Jewish or Scotch who would understand her & then she would be heroically good. She would be happy with children I think. Once she gets over the all for enjoyment-period & see [sic] that the unselfish life is the life of greatest happiness come what may. If she will not go to the Arts Student's League. Perhaps she would join you in your business. Can do is easily carried all constructive work for humain [sic] beings is worth doing.

There is an actress Miss Rosemary Carver going to New York on the 14th Aug or 21st Aug. She could escort Peggy Jean, and also take the painting Mr Epstein & I want you to have. This Rosemary Carver is known to your cousin Abner Dean I believe. . .

[FOURTH PAGE]

. . . In desperation at seeing the young life given up to enjoyment only, I got Miss Betty Joel a good friend of mine to take Peggy Jean into her Beauty Correspondence business "Ignes [sic] Slimming Salts Ltd"

*Epstein's son Jackie, born in September, 1934.

She has been working with her some months quite well, but it does not prevent the sturdy little desperado from dancing till 6 in the morning all the same, then sleeping 3 hours & then going to business. She promises to lead a new life if I let her go to you. She says herself sometimes she has had enough, but she is rumba [sic] mad & can't refuse invitations I'm afraid & the coloured clubs are too open here & too near in fact all

[FIFTH PAGE]

over the place & increasing overnight like mushrooms All that terrific energy might be going to painting & drawing & music or even dress making though she says she could never be able to? anything constructive. You see what I mean, she needs a new bent & influence. She likes communal effort at least of 2 – She could never be a lone wolf.

. . . Rosemary has a niece at the Art Students League. That would be good as a start. Peggy Jean would not go anywhere to start with alone, having been used always to go about with governesses.

[SIXTH PAGE]

With all her wild rumba work she is a timid little soul in a lot of things & ways.

She needs to finish her education, She might get it at the Art Students League I think. Education is only a matter of the influence of the people who surround you. The best school might be bad if their teachers were not a good influence. She tried Dartington Hall school. They taught her to smoke & drink at 13, among other things.

I feel that you and what you would choose for her would be good. I don't like to lose her but there's a rut here

Jacob feels when he comes home at 7 a. m. in the morning & he sees Peggy-Jean getting out of her taxi, in front of him by a ½ minute – that perhaps his life has influenced her. He feels this very much.

[SEVENTH PAGE]

That's why he has an idea of consenting to this scheme of her going to you for a while

He can't get out of his mix up in a hurry – but some day we might pick up the little Jacob and the 3 of us make a run for it, as we did in 1927

Then it failed but he had not quarrelled with her so much then but the next time it would succeed I think

Get hold of Joseph Ratner sometime next year (John J Hall Room) Columbia University and broach the subject of Epstein coming to America again.

He was simply magnificent the last time. He got Prof. John Dewey & Prof. Boas to sit and Mr. Clarence Darrow would have posed if Epstein had stayed.

[EIGHTH PAGE]

Mr J Ratner was a little fellow but he had gigantic ideas. It would have to be next year about June because Jacob is signed up for 2 exhibitions one Dec & one in April (So in Dec & Jan or June I could get square with you for P.J.)

So I would not worry Mr. Ratner till nearer then

I can imagine a string of portraits in New York & Washington could be arranged. This time I think Mr. Ratner should have a percentage of 10% at least to recompense him.

Then we might join you & Peggy-Jean. I'm scurrying through this letter when I'm supposed to be doing at *least 6 other things one gets so infernally busy in an artist's household when he runs 3 establishments* & the intake does not suffice for 1. Peggy-Jean has no idea of money either just like him. She always throws her bag in the farthest corner of the dance club so you should never give her more than 1 or 2 dollars or they take it.*

[ALONG LEFT SIDE MARGIN]

With love ever yours Peggy

Some day I shall be able to thank you for giving Peggy-Jean a lift & perhaps an impetus to art Here she is too near us

Peggy Jean was just over seventeen then. I couldn't blame Peggy Jean. Margaret and Jacob were always having blacks in their house. There was Paul Robeson, and there were others – doctors, lawyers, and actors. How was she to know? Peggy Jean came over in August and she stayed until October 1936. She came with the model of my brother's, Rosemary Carver. Miss Carver's mother was a very cultivated woman; she was head of the American Theater in Shanghai. Peggy Jean told me she hardly saw Miss Carver on the trip over; Rosemary Carver was always off somewhere. Well; this model comes down the gangplank and she's got a big, artificial monkey draped over her shoulders. I said to myself: "What kind of a thing is this?" I didn't know she was Peggy Jean's chaperone.

Rosemary comes up to me and she says: "Are you Aunt Sylvia?

I said: "Yes."

So she said: "I have this for you." And she handed me an envelope with seventy-five dollars in it. Expenses for Peggy Jean – good for about four days. Margaret never had any money. I lent them money; they never paid it back. You'd just have to forget about it.

Peggy Jean stayed with us in the Press apartment on 113th Street. Miss Carver went on to the Coast. I couldn't have put them both up; I didn't have any room. Peggy Jean slept on the day couch in the living room. Oh, was she a problem. She used to walk around the apartment in the nude – just like she did at home. She didn't know the difference, and my husband got very nervous. We had to stop that. Margaret wrote Peggy Jean letters that she shouldn't make a triangle between her uncle and aunt. Peggy Jean was unmanageable. She wouldn't come home at night. I'd get up in the morning and see the day couch empty. I was beside myself. All of sudden the phone would ring and it would be Peggy Jean. She'd say: "I stayed with the people you introduced me to, because it was too late to come home." I didn't know what she was doing and I had to think of my business. Margaret had no right to do that to me – that I should have such responsibility. I asked my brother Doc what to do.

He said: "Send her back. Send her back. You're going to have trouble with her." Peggy Jean didn't want to go back.

LETTER FROM MARGARET EPSTEIN TO SYLVIA PRESS
[Dated] 2 October 1936

South Kensington
SW7 London

---

*The three establishments were Epstein's two households and his home in Epping Forest.

Dear Sylvia
I have your letter of the 19th. Telegrams always cause wars

They can never say all they mean & always sound insolent.

Don't be worried about my cablegram. I had to write about what was in his mind when he opened and read your letter. I did it just to carry out his wishes at the moment as that always makes him calm down and as I explained writing letters at the moment was impossible. He just did not like to think of Peggy Jean incommodating you in the small flat. Then he is most awfully hard up at the moment and he had a fear that he would not be able to pay for Peggy Jean's stay in New York so I had to caution Peggy Jean through you about dress. He goes about in rags pretty much so do I as you have seen. We live such a busy life we never think of a stitch of clothes but Peggy Jean is a gay young thing and I try to get her what I can. She looks so well in pretty clothes but having about 10,000 dollars of debt here $3000 to money lenders gives one the staggers, when one stops to think of it which I try not to. However someday I shall be able perhaps to pay you back for helping Peggy Jean. I can quite see from your letter that you have got your share of troubles & I think it was heroic of you to offer to take Peggy Jean under the circumstances. She is absolutely I can see head over heels in love with New York & flatly refuses to leave it so I suppose she had better stay. So I am writing hurried gasps of letters to everyone I know there to see if they can get her a situation.

[SECOND PAGE]

I've been doing this for a month now as I know Peggy Jean would be difficult perhaps impossible to wrench away from New York. I've tried 5 or 6 people one of them I expect you Leane Zugsmith have met [sic]. She was always in our flat when we were at 38 W 59. She looked after storing of all the bronzes the 45 of them for Epstein in 1927-28 and she saw to the sending of the remnant back years later. She was a brick to us. She & Rose Lee who brought him a turkey.

As she Leane Zugsmith has always worked herself I thought she might be able to find a situation for Peggy Jean in the event of her not wanting to come back, I asked her to get in to touch with her & try & find out her suitability for a situation, and what could be done about it, but so far no suitable situation has turned up amongst any of the 5 or 6 people I have approached. Leane seemed the most possible because she was among books & publishers & people who might need someone to do easy work because Peggy Jean has never learned shorthand or much of typewriting, but I'm afraid it looks as if I was not going to succeed. I feel that as Peggy Jean has seemingly decided to make New York her home I must find her a niche or she will be unhappy if she has no work & no money coming regularly from here. She feels that you are spending too much on her I think, and she speaks of trying to get work. My trying to get her something to do from here is like trying to arrange something in Pekin. She does say in her last letter that you had something in the offing for her. Some situation I take it but she did not know if she could get it or what it was. That would occupy her mind & keep her from despairing about money till we can get her some. She must not feel too dependent

[THIRD PAGE]

that would hurt her. Yet under the circumstances it is difficult for her. Any work that she could get that would occupy her mind would be good to begin with. I must write to a lot more people. I must do it in the middle of the night I'm afraid. I'm so infernally busy. Peggy Jean does not want to come back. I would be quite agreeable if you or Leane could find her something to do to her staying in New York for a year. We would arrive there eventually I'm sure after this year. Certainly she wants to stay in New York, but how can it be managed?

There must be someone who could employ her there I could get her easily something here but she wants a change, & a change would be good for her if it could be done cheaply. I must think. Time is short. Every-

thing is expensive. I must write to some publishers if they can get her a job. When you are not there at home encourage her to go to Leane. It would cheer her & encourage her to see anyone who works as hard as Leane and is so angelic about it and that would help her to find her way about New York. I know she has been introduced to all the family friends & everybody by you. That was most good of you. Can any of them find her something to do. Surely that should be most easy for some of the people who are not working as hard as you and Leane are. Now that she does not want to go to the Art Students League and she wishes to stay, the only way will be for her to get some work to do, and if she does not like the first job, perhaps she could get a better & teach herself typewriting & practice shorthand perhaps, but you will be more able to judge what she can do there more than I can by a long chalk.

[FOURTH PAGE]

Epstein has calmed down now that I sent off his wishes in a wise cablegram and says the best thing for Peggy Jean if she stays is for her to get a situation "as she does not want to go to my old school" he says. He is not angry with me about it her going to New York I mean any more. His rages go off like a child's, but he opens every letter with a New York stamp on it all the same just as if they were his own. It's about my Peggy Jean, he thinks & he just opens them the darling! That shows he is anxious about her. I never seem to reach them first (the letters) try as hard as I can to race him.

Well, letter writing does not affect things very quickly when you think that the letter from Peggy Jean written 21st Sept. has just come in an hour ago & this one will reach you about the 12 of Oct.

I'm writing in the dark almost so as not to waken him. He has been asleep for hours. The Macys I mentioned Leane knows him, Mr. Macy in my telegram have probably not reached New York yet. They were going from London to New York a week ago when I saw them or him rather I saw & then he & his wife are packing up their goods & children & coming back here to stay for some time early in October he planned to get back. They will look up Peggy Jean I expect.

I must get his address & get the news to him that Peggy Jean does not want to get back & ask him if he knows of a situation for her there. Its not easy for Peggy Jean to get a situation for outside Betty Joel's establishment she has had no experience or preparation. Well I'd better get to bed its 2 a.m. & I must get up at 7 a.m. Do the best you can for us. She has had an unusually stormy upbringing I will try to repay you for it. & needs unusual assistance in some ways. Ever yours always with love & best wishes.

[Signed]

Peggy

Margaret had so much to do – and she had to take care of him – Jacob. She was in a daze, the poor thing. Her letters are all mixed up – a *megillah*. But, I just could not take Peggy Jean on. I would put up the money for her education; it would not be paid back. I did what I could to help. I sent them money and I was always sending Peggy Jean clothes, but this was their responsibility, not mine.

Peggy Jean was sent back in October with some new clothes, and I got a letter from Margaret thanking me for my help. Peggy Jean worked for a while at Foyle's, but she did not want to be there. She wanted to be in New York, so Margaret, Jacob and Peggy Jean went on a holiday. They took her to Paris. I suppose Jackie, who was born in 1934, was left home with a nurse. Peggy Jean told me she came home from private school one day and the baby was there. He had been born in London and Margaret had taken him over after birth. Anyway, to get Peggy Jean's mind off New York, they were in Paris and they were sitting at one of those outdoor, sidewalk cafes. This young fellow, Norman Hornstein, comes up and asks Peggy Jean if she would like to go to listen to Hungarian music. He was

American and he was studying medicine at the University in Edinburgh.

My sister-in-law said: "Young man, come here. What do you want?" He told her that he wanted to take Peggy Jean to the concert. Margaret says: "Well, it's just too bad. We're going home tomorrow and she can not go."

They left and he followed them back to London. He courted Peggy Jean, and proposed to her. Her picture was in the London newspapers announcing her engagement and they were married when she was eighteen years old.

Jacob liked Norman. According to Margaret, he liked him better than Peggy Jean's other suitors, but there were difficulties which arose. Norman posed for two portrait busts, and he also posed for the angel in *Jacob and the Angel*. Then World War Two came and he was in the British Army. Peggy Jean had two children by then, Ian and Leda. She visited Norman whenever she could. She told me that one time she was going to see her husband, and at the last minute she decided to take both children along. Ian was a baby, and she took him with her. When she returned from the visit, her house had been destroyed by the German bombings.

LETTER FROM MARGARET EPSTEIN TO SYLVIA PRESS

Telephone Western 5723

18 Hyde Park Gate
SW7
13/10/37

Dear Sylvia

Knowing Peggy Jean's powers of correspondence I'm lifting my weary pen from addressing a 1000 of these to put you on her tracks

She has married an American

A New Yorker

She is happy
She is at The Dell
  Dell Road
  Colinton
  Edinburgh

He is very good for her I think

[ALONG RIGHT SIDE MARGIN]

Thanking you for your care of her
She took all my time up from Jackie
& hubby. Now I have a new son to
look after her half & half.
We are partners in it.

[SECOND PAGE]

Peggy Jean would not go to a finishing school in Brussels and she would not go to a school for domestic science they did not mean a thing to her. Well now she's got the real thing. He's not a man of money in fact he's a student but then all the men of money are spoiled by having hundreds of women after them. Much more good at the catching men game than P.J. could be and that chasing of hundreds just spoil these men with money. Men of title have thousands of women after them and that makes them insane as husbands. It's best to be philosophical. Peggy Jean does not hanker after furs and jewels. She has a chance of happiness with this man I think at first I was afraid he was too beautiful but Communism has been his religion and that has kept him good I think.

He is studying hard now and some day you will see them both in New York I'm sure. He likes America best and he is one of those husbands who gets what he wants within reason. He's the only one of Peggy Jean's admirers that Epstein really liked.

All the best wishes
and love
from

Peggy
[Signed]

CHAPTER TWELVE

I put my husband in business three times. Three times it went *mechuleh*. It wasn't a bankruptcy but it was bad. I had to close out my dress company, and I went out of business after eight years, in 1938. I stopped working and a buyer from Lord & Taylor's called me up. Her name was Nettie Hartsell and she was a very big buyer. I used to sell her over $100,000 a year. Nettie wants to see me. She says: "You mean to tell me that you're going to stay at home? A girl like you? You've got so much on the ball."

I said: "Well, I don't know how to look for a job."

Nettie says: "Well, I'm going to call Mr. Ben Lindner and find out whether or not he can use you." So she did. She said: "How would you like Sylvia Epstein to work for you?" No one called me anything but Sylvia Epstein. I was never called Sylvia Press, even after I was married, and Al didn't like that much.

Mr. Lindner said: "Oh, I would love it. Send her over." He already had a girl working for him and I didn't want to be in the middle; I didn't want to take her job away. She was there when I came and when she saw me she almost took a fit. I went into Mr. Lindner's private office.

"Oh, I don't want to take her job", I said.

Mr. Lindner said: "She's threatening me all the time and I'm sick and tired of it. I want you to come in Monday."

So I went there, to 1400 Broadway, and I did the same kind of work, saleswoman and designer of popular-priced dresses. I stayed there for a few years. The War came on and we still made clothes, using synthetics to make up for shortages in materials. We never made uniforms, although there was one man in our building, I think his name was Cohn – he made them. After a few years I left Lindner's and I worked for another man, making $200 a week. I designed for The New Look, and we did the long-skirted suit with the pinched-in waists. Around 1955, I retired for good. Do you know, I went on the road and sold? Every week I used to drive to Philadelphia, Baltimore, and Washington. I sold Hutzler's in Baltimore and Garfinckel's in Washington, and I used to know those towns so well.

Al was not good as a salesman. He was a vain man, very handsome, and he wanted all the attention for himself. He was very jealous also. Now, he knew I was the brains of the business and still he made me get out. Those Presses – they were something. Al had two uncles who were congenitally blind. They were on his mother's side, and there had been a marriage of two first cousins. First I lived with my mother-in-law, and later Al and I had our own apartment. It is the one I have today. All the furniture in it – I bought. Al's mother, Sophie, lived with us. That's why we had to have an extra bedroom and another bath. She lived with us for nineteen years; then she went to the Coast and she wanted me to support her in a hotel on the Coast. Mrs. Press was gorgeous, with beautiful skin and black eyes. She treated Al shabbily. Her favorite was the other son, Lou, who was two-and-a-half years older than Al. She liked Lou because he was a nothing. Lou was in the garment trade and he had several wives.

Divorce was not looked down upon in the garment industry. My women friends often were divorced; they married again, and it was not the great scandal it was outside New York at that time. But Lou – he had women who ran around a lot too. I know because I visited his second wife once, in Palm Springs. She told me another woman took him away from her, but I don't know – she had a lot of other men friends too. Lou died when Al was sick at Long Island Jewish Hospital and I was afraid to tell him. Lou had left an insurance policy to me. He had borrowed on it, because Lou borrowed from everybody, and took from everybody. There was about $900 left on the policy after the loan was paid off, and when I told Al, he said: "He left a policy to *you?*" Well, I supported his mother and I was always lending Lou money.

Al said: "My God in Heaven, he was just put out of a hotel, and I paid to get his clothes out."

I said: "Al, whatever you want – you can have." So he took $250 to cover his losses.

Al had gone into the brokerage business, after we lost the business. There was a bar in the building where I had my business, and a man who was a stockbroker used to come in there. He said: "You know, Al, you'd make a marvelous stockbroker. I'm going to become assistant manager at Hentz & Company. When I do, I want you to come up and see me, because you know everybody. Everybody talks to you and you talk to everybody and that's what we need in this business."

Al was hesitant to go. I said: "What have you got to lose? It's better than walking around, doing nothing. Go up – see." Al went up there and the head manager talked to him.

He said: "How much business can you bring in?"

Al said: "I don't know if I can bring in a hundred dollars or a million dollars worth of business. I don't know what I can do. I've never been in this business."

The manager said; "Well, I like the way you talk." So he took him on, and, of course, in that business, you've got to prove yourself – to get a salary. You have to work six months and then take an examination. Al brought in the first month, from one man alone, $50,000-worth of business. My friends Eva Burke and Ralph Krause were afraid to start with him – they didn't know, for Al had never been in the business. Al was very friendly with men, and he always could get a lot of women around him. These god-damned men – they'd sell their souls for a woman. Al did very well; in those days he was making about $25,000 a year and I was working too.

Hentz & Company was a Jewish firm. I remember old man Hentz from when I was a child. He lived in Yorkville. Al did well there, but he finally had to leave because one of the managers would take Al's business and give it to himself. Al was not getting credit for it, so he left there and went to another firm; it was a Gentile firm, but I don't now remember the name. Al stayed there until he died in 1969, and he did very well there too.

After I retired in 1955 or so, I used to drive Al into work every day, but I never took him back. He had a car and chauffeur to bring him home. Al was ill by that time – he had lung trouble. Later, he had a car and chauffeur drive him both ways. He'd come home and say to me: "Everybody says to me: 'What's your wife doing? Why doesn't she come back? I've got a job for her.'"

My friend Eva said to me: "If you go back, you'll work for the rest of your life. Don't you *dare* go back to work."

Sophie Press was not very nice to me. She was always talking about me. I worked, and I had a maid to come in and do the housework. One day I came in, and I overheard Sophie on the telephone. She was saying: "Of course, she's been married before." She was talking about me. I had never been married before. Would I lie about a thing like that? One day we were all sitting at the breakfast table, eating, and she said something to me. I got so angry that I slammed my coffee cup down on the saucer. It broke and I cut my little finger nearly off. I ran into the bedroom, crying, and Al ran after me.

He said: "Sweetheart, I know – don't tell me about my mother." The finger was treated, but it has been crooked ever since. Finally Mrs. Press broke her hip and had to be put in a nursing home. I couldn't take care of her anymore, but Al would not go to see her. I was the one who visited her.

The only one of my family that Al really liked was my niece Marthe. Marthe's father, Harold, was a very kind, lovely man. He was a dentist, but he was also an inventor, scientist, businessman, and amateur sculptor. Harold invented and patented a synthetic rubber process during World War II and he experimented a great deal with dental materials. He also did fine amateur sculpture. I sit in my apartment now, and around me I see his work – a bronze head of Einstein, and his bas reliefs of his brother, Sir Jacob Epstein. Marthe also has a lovely bronze of her mother, Naomi – very Rodinesque, and very good. Harold used to say that he only did famous men and beautiful women. I also have a harlequin statue by my niece Marthe and a few fine prints and drawings by her son, Marc. As I said, we are a family of artists. When Harold died in 1961, he left his bronzes to his wife, and after her death a year later, Marthe, following her father's and mother's wishes, gave Al and me some of Harold's work. Al was very touched. He couldn't get over it. He said: "It's the first time in my life I ever got something for nothing."

I have never been much of a collector of my brother Jacob's work. I have the watercolor of roses sent to me as a wedding present, and in 1949 Marthe brought me back a large pencil drawing of Jackie, which Jacob sent to me*. In the late 1930s Margaret and Jacob asked me to be Jacob's agent here in America. Jacob had had such trouble with agents that he didn't want anyone he didn't trust to represent him, but I couldn't take it on and work at my business. I said to Doc: "You take it. You can manage your own time." My brother, Dr. Irving Epstein, became his agent in America and stayed his agent until Jacob died in 1959.

I did buy one lovely bronze directly from Jacob. It was a little Berber child's head, the *Tabitha*. I bought it in 1958. Jacob sold his bronzes to our family for what he had to spend to have them cast. Jacob sent me a letter** telling me how pleased he was that I was to be listed among his collectors. Jacob was very fond of that piece; you see, he used to do things like his children's heads for pleasure, but he remarked in his letter to me that he had very little time for that, since his time was all taken up with large commissions for buildings and churches. He said that his health was somewhat better, but that he had to slow down. Jacob suffered from heart disease. He was looking forward to another visit with us the following year, but he died and this was the last letter I ever received from him. Jacob remarked in the letter that he felt it to be so odd that while he received all kinds of commissions from Christian churches and cathedrals, the only synagogue which wanted to commission his work was one down in Dallas and they would not offer enough to pay for the casting. This, he said, from a wealthy congregation.

Al would never go anywhere after we were married. I think he travelled to the Coast once and came back through the Panama Canal, but he would not travel and he did not want me to travel either. I loved to travel, and so, when I went anywhere, I'd go with my girl friends, without Al. Once I went to Tijuana, Mexico, and I used to go to Palm Springs a lot. I drove a car, and we'd go to a resort where they had whirlpool baths, the hot and cold baths, you know. I visited Lou's ex-wife and people on the Coast. Once, while I was on the Coast, after I bought the *Tabitha*, Al took it and sold it without my permission. When I got back, I was furious. He *sold* it, without my *permission*. He had no right to do that. It was sold to members of my friend Eva's family; I tried to get it back – offered them what they paid for it – but they would not sell it. Why didn't I get it back legally? Ah, I didn't want to start in with him. You couldn't do anything with Al; you couldn't reason with him. I asked him why he did it. He said: "Well, I can take that money and invest it – make more from it." He sold it for a small price and it is worth a lot more today.

In 1931 my brother Lou died. His son, Abner, graduated from Dartmouth that same year. Lou was a lovely, quiet man. He never lived to see Abner's career as a cartoonist. Ida died in 1951. In 1947 Margaret Epstein died, but she had been active up to the end, always arranging shows for Jacob. Margaret had a stroke in a London cab and fell out – that was the end. Peggy Jean was living in America by then. My husband would not let me go with her to the funeral. When she came back, Peggy Jean told me: "It's just too bad that you didn't go with me to Mummy's funeral. They had one

*Mrs. Press also owned the third signed copy of the Churchill, and a Nehru. She was afraid of robbery and would not allow this to be printed during her lifetime.
**Sir Jacob Epstein to Sylvia Press, August 23, 1958

room upstairs – a bedroom – which was so full of her collection of art and things, that something had fallen across the door and they couldn't open it. It was all full of vermin and mold when they later opened it. If you'd been there, you'd have known what to take. I didn't know." Later they threw everything out. My niece Marthe told me about that room. She saw it when she was there. There was a bust of John Dewey on the floor, completely covered in cobwebs.

LETTER FROM MARGARET EPSTEIN TO SYLVIA PRESS, WRITTEN SOMETIME DURING THE WEEK BEGINNING DECEMBER 14, 1941 (letter is not dated)

Dear Sylvia,
You sent a sweet telegram of concern at the beginning of the war and much as we felt it we just couldn't answer. The book* has been the only subject and thought day & night till end of last week when the U.S. went in. Dr Irving was kind enough to send photographs I'm not quite sure if I have his last address, I thought we heard of his moving, and the New York phone books Hiram Halle sends me stopped with the 1936. I am writing to thank Irving

I believe the curtain Jacob did for the ballet of David and Goliath is going to America this next week, to Dolin, so you might be able to see it if Dolin is dancing. Dolin I believe is trying to sell it.

ALONG RIGHT MARGIN
Everyone is selling here what is not rivetted (sic) to their person Rockefeller Centre is about the kind of place that would have space to hang it. The owner is a Mrs Laura Henderson here in London.

Peggy-Jean, Norman Hornstein, her husband and Leda their baby are at "Pykara" Westfields, Whiteleaf, Monks Risborough, Buckinghamshire where he is billeted with his hospital unit for the time of the

SECOND PAGE
duration of the war.
The baby is very like her father, a very long baby. She is as intelligent as a much much (sic) older baby generally is, and she is going to be a good looker. She is steadily gaining in weight and laughs loud and long. They dote on her of course. They are quite happy. They never have a penny but thats better than getting stale and blasé & disatisfied (sic) from having too much, which is often seen in London. They will get more money someday but they and Leda will never be more good looking or happier than they are now.

Peggy-Jean works so very hard "washy washing dry dry" for Leda and cooking for Norman and looking after the house that she never has time to write to anyone but that's better than dancing all night & sleeping all day as she once did.

She would love you to write to her and she keeps asking me for your last address.

I must look under the tons of debris of the book for that, I seem to remember that your last letter came from a holiday resort. That would not find you.

THIRD PAGE
I must have a search to see what I can find in the way of address and send it on to her, but with the best wish in the world I think she is too dead beat to write when Leda has finished. With her, Leda needs some

---
*Epstein's *Let There Be Sculpture*

attention, and she has to look after Norman, and he needs about 6 ft of attention. I will send this letter to the address I think is your latest and say please forward. Then I will write and thank Dr Irving for the photographs and find what I judge to be his latest address and send it to him "address not certain" please forward.

Perhaps you will think this funny but the fact is all filing of letters, bills, and receipts etc at once stopped being done when the book really got into swing in Sept so there is a pile for me to get in to in the new year and it will be some time before I can clear it & find everything.

Some little disputes will go on with the publishers – there must often be such I suppose but I think the book will be out in the spring Feb. or March if not before

The publisher is not very intelligent which is a pity, but we chose him because he offered more money than the others

FOURTH PAGE

However we haven't seen the money yet, we had hoped to before Xmas but alas there is no sign of it yet. We found that the war cut in and smashed all the contracts connected with Adam, which were so much advertised, so we are not at all well off at the moment, still something always seems to turn up in the nick of time, so I never worry.

Peggy-Jean & Norman are joining us up in London at Xmas or at the cottage near by in Epping Forest 50 Baldwin's Hill Loughton. Tel Loughton 624 for Xmas day. Our little Jackie is dying to know what name Norman has given to the Alsatian puppy some one has presented him with. I understand they are seen in the streets of Aylesbury Bucks. Peggy-Jean carrying Leda and Norman carrying His Highness the Alsatian pup who is supposed to be of a champion breed. I myself don't approve of the proximity of dogs especially Alsatian and babies but I'm supposed to be old fashioned and fussy so I'm philosophic & say nothing. Nothing really teaches but experience.

Our little Jackie is fast growing up big. He is 4 stones and 4 feet and is very like Jacob. He has the same kind of blue eyes and the same cheeks and the same hands. He is I suppose what Jacob was when he was little a terrible mixture of goodness & bad moods, highly strung, a temper like a volcano one moment, and sweet & good hearted the next curiously enough only interested in machinery and ships. Engines are his little Jackie's heart's delight.

He thinks of a submarine as a paradise.

FIFTH PAGE

If we can get some money we may leave London for a bit – and go to some land not in the war world. I don't know exactly where he wants to go yet. Somewhere where he can work & where he has the models he wants. Then when he had enough for an exhibition he would hie to New York I think. That's always the question when he had money he has not the work for to hold an exhibition with, and when he has the works all ready, he seldom has the money for the journey and all connected with it. I hope you are having a happy time and having luck in business. Here the business has all come to a standstill. The news is very meagre compared to the million a minute expense. I wish it could be got over and done with and construction of normal life proceeded with again instead of this sinister gloomy destruction. Of course Hitler must be stopped far be it for a fighting race like mine to funk the battle over – but the waste of life and what is needed for the lives of the poor especially, that is appalling to think of. If only someone near him (Hitler) could see to it that his life only was forfeit, as it should be, and perhaps by a heroic act save all those who will otherwise be slaughtered next year perhaps.

SIXTH PAGE

The book will cause a lot of discussion Not very good tempered discussion Im afraid but it will sell all the better for a "bonnie fecht" to begin with.

You will see it soon.

I will send you a copy as "to the most charming of all the Epstein's to me in New York Louis"* I must not, not ever forget how he supplied us with luxuries in every way, and helped where he could. What a pity he was finished off so soon. He plied us with eats like marvellous cakes and pies. A supply arrived after we had gone & had to be sent back to shop. I regret that happened but Jacob cannot endure commoness (?) like good boys. God rest his soul. He was a gentle unselfish loving spirit. Best wishes to all Epsteins. I was a silent observer in 1928 and 1927 (Oct. 1927 – Jan. 27 1928). We Scotch people are slow thinkers but we never forget.

With love from
Margaret
[Signed]

P.S. I think Jacob will be doing the Lloyd George early in the New Year.

*Louis Epstein. 1927 visit to America.

Plate 37: *The Bowater House Group, Hyde Park, London (Jacob Epstein, bronze, 1959)*

Plate 38: *Moon God*, 2nd-3rd century AD, stone, Temple of Bel, Palmyra, Syria

Plate 39: *Oscar Wilde Tomb* (detail)

Plate 40: *The Jacob Bigelow Sphinx*, Mt Auburn Cemetery, Cambridge, Mass (Martin Milmore, granite 1872)

The text carved on the monument reads:

AMERICAN UNION PRESERVED
AFRICAN SLAVERY DESTROYED
BY THE UPRISING OF A GREAT PEOPLE
BY THE BLOOD OF FALLEN HEROES

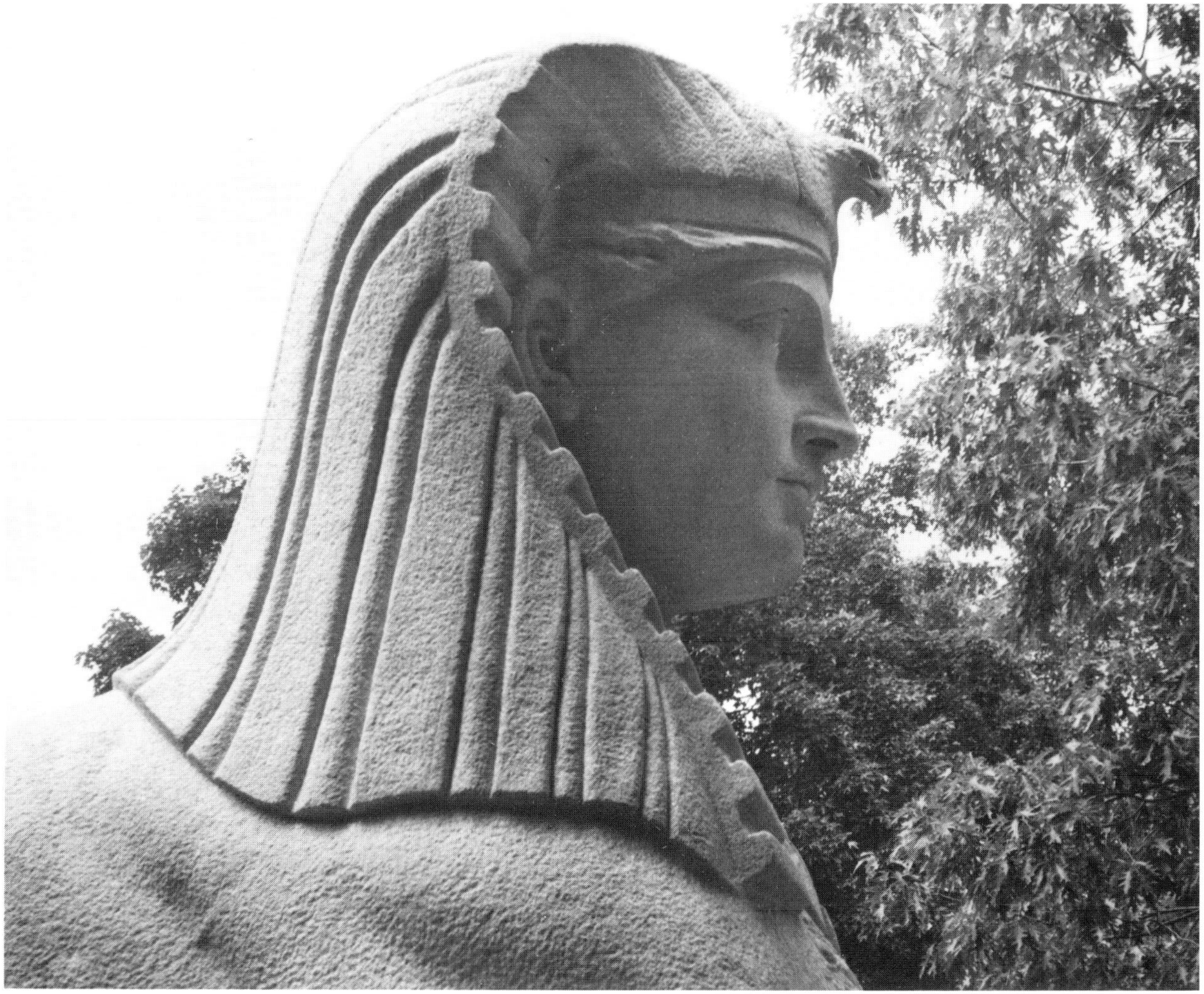

Plate 41: *The Jacob Bigelow Sphinx* (detail)

Plate 42: *The Adams Memorial,* Rock Creek Cemetery, Washington D.C. (Augustus Saint-Gaudens, bronze, 1891)

Plate 43: *The Adams Memorial*

Plate 44: *The Adams Memorial* (detail)

Plate 45: *The Visitation,* The Hirshhorn Museum and Sculpture Garden

Plate 46: *The Visitation*, The Hirshhorn Museum and Sculpture Garden

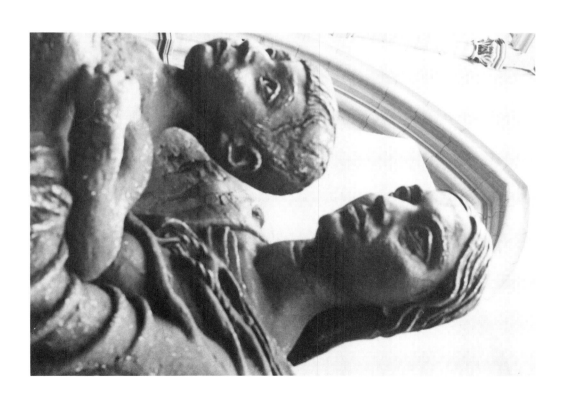

Plate 48: *The Charioteer of Delphi*, bronze, c470 BC, Delphi Museum, Delphi, Greece (detail)

CHAPTER THIRTEEN

Sunita left Jacob's home and disappeared sometime in the 1930s, I believe. She took up with an Englishman, who refused to marry her. Sunita died a suicide.

My father, Max Esptein, lived to be eighty-three years old. We all helped support him and in his last years he lived at Chana's. He died on June 25, 1941. Chana died at eighty-one on January 7, 1966. She is also buried in Washington Cemetery, in Brooklyn.

Jerry Solomon, Chana's son, became an important business executive. He also handled some of the disposal and sale of Jacob's art after my brother's death. Jerry knew Lady Kathleen well, and upon the death of Sally Fortune Ryan he assisted Lady Kathleen with the dispersal of Miss Ryan's large art collection. Sally Fortune Ryan had studied with Jacob and was a friend of my brother's as well as a friend of his second wife. Jacob liked Miss Ryan very much. She owned a varied collection of art and bought my brother's work. Jacob's *The Sun God,* first started in 1910 and completed in 1933, was owned by Miss Ryan and was exhibited in her garden at her estate in Redding, Connecticut until her death. I understand that *The Sun God* is now in the basement of The Metropolitan Museum of Art in New York. Through Jerry's efforts a number of Epstein's pieces have been placed in collections in the United States. Jerry died in 1976, shortly before we began this book.

* * * * * *

In 1939 I wrote the Myron Selznick Company about an idea I had for a movie on Jacob Epstein's life. I received a letter from a Mr. Collier Young saying that they might be interested but the War came and the idea was scrapped. Jacob would never have allowed it anyway. I'd also talked to Metro-Goldwyn-Mayer and they wanted to give me $5000 for an outline, but my husband Al said: "Oh, no. My wife doesn't give any outline." He knew about the movie business.

Around 1941 or so I went to The New School for Social Research and took a writing course. The teacher was a writer, a Jewish fellow. When he heard my brother was Jacob Epstein – oh – ! I said: "Please don't tell anybody." I was in a class, writing, with a lot of adults you know. Everything I wrote he thought was wonderful.

He'd say: "Oh, this is beautiful". When I graduated at the end of the semester, he had a dinner party for us. He gave the party and he said to the class: "We have a very outstanding woman here whom I've never told you about. She comes from a very famous family. There are famous people in her family and I must tell you who they are. His name is Jacob Epstein and Sylvia Press is her name". I still have the letter the teacher wrote to me, asking me to the party and asking me what I intended to wear to it.

There was one woman in this class. She was a writer and a *meshuggeneh.* She was an artist too. My husband used to warn me against her because she used to call me up all the time. She'd say: "Can't you ever get away from your husband?" Al used to be afraid she was queer. The teacher in my writing class used to write too; he'd get ballet tickets and couldn't I ever get away from my husband.

* * * * * *

During the bombing of London in World War Two, Jacob exhibited a beautiful, carved, white gardenia. He also made lots of drawings of gardenias and other flowers, including sunflowers. His last portrait of Esther, a bronze, represents her dressed to go out with a gardenia at her breast. During the war people asked why he did such a mild symbol at a time like that. He said: "With the world at war, why create more tension?" I don't know what the gardenia meant – purity maybe.

Jacob always loved Peggy Jean so much. He told me that when he was working on the bust of Conrad, he found Conrad to be very exacting-from the people around him. Jacob sent for Peggy Jean then. After Jacob and Augustus John fell out, Epstein disliked John very much. He was always afraid John was going to kidnap Peggy-Jean. You see, John liked little girls.

Jackie was always a favorite of Jacob's but Jacob and Theo did not get along well. Kitty was very extravagant – she used to run up big department store bills, but Jacob always indulged her – whatever she wanted. Esther was loved dearly, I believe, although I never saw the other children. I have never seen Kitty or her children by her first husband, Lucien Freud. I have heard about them. Lucien Freud, a grandson of Sigmund Freud, is a well-known painter today. His daughter, Annabel Freud, was the model for the baby in the carriage on Epstein's bas-reliefs below *The Liverpool Giant. The Liverpool Giant* is a huge bronze, a young male statue standing on a boat, over the entrance doorways to Lewis's Department Store in Liverpool, England. Epstein's dog Frisky is the model for the dog beside the baby in the carriage.

Marthe met the Garman children when she visited at her uncle's home in 1949 and 1951. In 1951 Esther and her mother were at the house and Epstein took them all to dinner at the Café Royal. At that time Marthe saw some of Theo's painting. She told me that it was very fine, and he had an expressionistic style, somewhat like Matisse. In 1952, or around that time, Esther committed suicide after an unhappy love affair. She had left the house at Hyde Park Gate and had moved into her own apartment. Jacob had helped her with the apartment, but she could not overcome her depression. She was still a very young girl when she died. In 1954 Theo committed suicide in Italy, where he lived. He had been ill a long time and was diagnosed as a schizophrenic. After her two children's deaths, Lady Kathleen converted to Catholicism.

Jackie Epstein used to be interested in motors and in racing motorcycles, but he has married a Catholic girl, now has children, and lives somewhere outside of London.

In 1954 my brother Jacob was knighted by Queen Elizabeth II. He had become a British subject in 1911, and when asked about how he felt about his British citizenship, he always told me that he regarded himself as an American who became a British subject. Jacob bought himself a new homburg and a long-tailed coat; he dressed up very elegantly for the ceremony. He was always elegant in his appearance, although he often wore baggy, unpressed, old suits. He never looked messy, but always special. Jacob told me that the only trouble was, after he was knighted, his tipping had to go up.

Peggy Jean and Norman had moved to America after World War Two. Norman came first and Peggy Jean followed later with the two children. Jacob bought them a home down in Buxton, North Carolina, on Cape Hatteras. Peggy Jean still owns the home; she rents it out and she has invested in real estate. She has become a very good businesswoman. Norman opened an office and infirmary. Peggy Jean worked in it with him. She wrote me once about the work there. Norman treated Coast Guard families as well as the islanders. Peggy Jean remarked in her letter, which was written in January, 1951, that she had gone off the island for the first time since last February and how she enjoyed seeing the people and the shops. She also remarked that her father was very worried about Jackie; he was afraid that he would be called up for service in the Korean War, but that didn't happen. Peggy Jean wrote about delivering twins – how she had assisted her husband as they only had a nurse in the mornings for operations. Peggy Jean had to do the night nursing, for the day nurse had small children and was unable to come.*

Jacob and Jackie visited the Hornsteins right after the War and I have a letter from Jacob describing the beaches there and how he enjoyed them. He didn't like the drudgery which Peggy Jean had there, always nursing, cooking and cleaning up. He said she needed something more cheerful, as she was a bright, gay person. Jacob liked gay, cheerful, people. That's why he liked me, I think. I was

---

*Peggy Jean Hornstein to Sylvia Press, January 11, 1951.

always gay – singing and dancing. Jacob talked about how isolated the island was and how unhelpful the islanders were about work. He was very pessimistic about Peggy Jean's marriage, but said that he didn't like to interfere and it was best to say nothing.**

Peggy Jean and Norman were divorced in 1957. Peggy Jean later married again and now lives in Long Beach, North Carolina. Jacob was very helpful to her after her divorce and up to his death; he always helped all of his children whenever he could. No one was cut out of his will either, like Picasso did to his children.

Jacob came over to America before 1954 to examine the site at Fairmount Park in Philadelphia for his American Group, the *Social Consciousness*. He came again for the dedication in 1954 and, oh, they had a big celebration when it was unveiled. They had a dinner in his honor and a big parade. My husband would not let me go. I cried and cried. Jacob came to see me on his way home and told me about it. "It was really something," he said. He was very pleased with his reception and the reaction to his work. I had a party at Long Beach, Long Island, for Jacob.

Jacob used to tell me stories about his sitters and the famous people he met. One of the people in America whom he liked was Helena Rubinstein. He never did her portrait, but he knew her very well. Jacob used to have her go to the different galleries and bid on things for him. He'd tell her to bid to a certain price and if the bid went over, she should stop bidding. So she'd go and she'd buy them for herself because it was more than he wanted to pay. He liked her. She bought a lot of his art. And it's funny – I knew a man who used to be a manager at her salon. His wife I knew very well, and, shortly before Helena Rubinstein died, this woman says to me: "Sylvia, Helena Rubinstein has invited you to come and visit her."

I thought to myself: "She knew my brother very well. What does she want with me?" I never went to see her.

Epstein thought that Gertrude Whitney was a big fake. He said that she didn't do her own sculpture. She would have other artists do things and put her name on the work. Jacob couldn't stand that.

Jacob lived right across the street from Winston Churchill on Hyde Park Gate. Epstein's famous bust of Churchill was done in 1947, and Churchill would not pose for very many sittings, so it wasn't finished. Jacob had dealt with the House of Marlborough before when he made the bust of the Duke of Marlborough in 1923-1925. The Duke's second wife, Gladys Deacon, was an American beauty and a friend of my brother's. Jacob told me he could not stand the way the Duke treated his wife. He treated her so badly that Jacob stopped work on the bust for two years. He didn't want to finish it, but he had already started it, and so he finally did.

Winston Churchill, said Jacob, was a very impatient man. They were neighbors, of course, and really, I think, friendly enemies. Churchill always referred to my brother as "that talented monster." Churchill used to receive cases of liquor free, as gifts, and he would never give my brother any at all. That annoyed Jacob.

Marthe and Allan Clamage met Winston Churcill in 1951. Marthe had brought her fiancé to her Uncle Jacob's house and they were having tea when there was a big commotion in the street outside. Marthe asked what it was, and Jacob said disgustedly: "Oh, *that man* is going out." Winston Churchill. Well, Marthe and Allan wanted to see him and so they asked to be excused, which Jacob granted, not too graciously. Winston Churchill was to come out of his house and although he was no longer prime minister, he still had a bodyguard. Marthe and Allan wanted a picture and so they asked the bodyguard for permission and he asked who they were. Marthe told him she was Jacob's niece and the bodyguard granted it, provided she took his picture first. This was to prevent an attack on Churchill by a camera gun. They snapped the picture but that meant that they had only one chance to photograph Churchill since there was only one exposure left on the film. Winston

---

**Sir Jacob Epstein to Sylvia Press, July 29th, no year listed, believed to be 1952.

Churchill came out and asked who they were. When he was told, he said: "Oh, *that man.*" He meant my brother. He shook hands with Marthe and Allan and they were shocked at the limp, feeble handshake and how old he appeared. He stepped back into the shadows and they snapped the picture, but the light was not too good, and the only thing they got was a shadowy image of the great man. He then stepped into his limousine and drove off, with all the official flags flying.

Jacob liked Marthe because he said she reminded him of his mother, Mary Epstein. Marthe, like Epstein's daughter Kitty, has the Epstein face. (Although a lot of our relatives resemble Mary Epstein, only Kitty in Jacob's family looks like his mother.)

Marthe asked her uncle about Churchill. Jacob was disgusted with the large amounts of money and publicity Churchill got for his painting. Jacob considered his art to be very bad. Epstein also talked to Marthe about his rivalry with Lipchitz for commissions for synagogues and temples. Marthe had met members of the Eric Gill family shortly before visiting her uncle, and had visited in the family home where Eric Gill had designed his own personal chapel. Gill was in competition with Epstein for commissions for churches and cathedrals. Jacob did not particularly criticize Gill's art, but he did feel that Gill's conversion to Catholicism was one reason he got a lot of his commissions. Jacob never renounced his Judaism. Epstein also told Marthe that he wanted his plaster molds of his sculpture to be given to the British Museum after his death. You see, he did his research there. He also wanted to stop any unauthorized editions of his work after his death. When Esther died, Jacob stopped all further castings from her last portrait mold. He said that never again would he make another bronze from that mold. Through Billy Rose's assistance after Epstein's death, Jacob's molds were given to Museum Israel in Jerusalem. Israel also has a few pieces by Jacob which are in the Tel-Aviv Art Museum, among which is a bust of Chaim Weizmann.

* * * * * *

The bust of Rabindranath Tagore was originally made with a halo over his head. Epstein at first considered Tagore to be a very holy and saintly man. Tagore was well-known for his philosophical writings. Sunita's son, Enver, came into the studio when Tagore was posing. The child went up to him, and Tagore shuddered, pulling his hand away from the child. Jacob saw it. Epstein said: "Oh!" And he ripped the halo off the sculpture. The bust was completed without the halo, as just a portrait.

Jacob told me that the first time George Bernard Shaw came to pose for him Shaw dropped all his clothes. Epstein said: "He had such an ugly body. I couldn't stand it."

Oh, Jacob did everybody. Haile Selassie came to the studio when he was in exile in London. Another person whom Jacob made a portrait of was Albert Einstein, who he said was a very gentle, soulful kind of man. Epstein also made a bust of the Italian actress, Gina Lollabrigida; he liked her very much.

Princess Margaret Rose posed for Jacob when she was a young woman. Princess Margaret was a bright, gay person and Jacob liked her at first but he had a lot of trouble with her. She got on his nerves. She was very bossy while she posed, and tried to tell him how she wanted herself represented. He said that if he hadn't had so much publicity with the bust, he would have stopped work on it. And they didn't like the hands on the portrait. Margaret had rather ordinary hands, and that's the way he showed them.

Epstein could be very humourous in his work. When Marthe was visiting in 1951, he was working on his portrait of Fannie Holtzmann, the famous international lawyer. Jacob had never owned his house at 18 Hyde Park Gate and the landlord wanted him to move. It was impossible for Jacob to do it; he had so much work to do that he'd have lost six months' time. He engaged Fannie Holtzmann to negotiate the lease. She fixed it so Jacob could remain there the rest of his life. Jacob asked her what she wanted in payment; she told him a portrait bust.

When she came to the studio to pose, she asked him: "Shall I strip to the waist?" Jacob told

Marthe he looked at her and told her that it was up to her. She was a rather plain woman, with a very intelligent face, and she wore false teeth. So she stripped and that's how he did her – a plain woman wearing her false teeth, with big, voluptuous breasts. When Marthe and Allan saw the portrait the first thing they said was: "But she's got false teeth." Jacob just smiled and said: "Yes, she has."

In 1956 Krushchev, Bulganin and Kurchatov visited England. I read about the time when they took Krushchev to visit Jacob in his studio in London. The newspapers wrote it up. They asked Krushchev what he thought of the art he saw there and Krushchev made some kind of stupid remark. Jacob said: "Well, you'd better stick to your murder. Go back to Russia and stick to your murder."

CHAPTER FOURTEEN

Jacob and Kathleen Garman were married in 1955. During the last few years of his life, my brother got some wonderful commissions. His great talent and genius were finally recognized. In 1955 he completed the Llandaff Cathedral commission for the aluminium *Christ in Majesty*. Jacob traveled there to see the church. It is an early Gothic cathedral* in Llandaff, Cardiff, Wales; he went and looked at the bombed-out roof and designed a beautiful Christ, which stands high up near the windows. It covers the organ. Jacob always loved music. In 1955 he also received a commission for the great *St. Michael and the Devil*, which is now on the wall outside the entranceway to the new Coventry Cathedral. Jacob completed this sculpture in 1958. *The Liverpool Giant* was also done during this period.

The old Coventry church, the St. Michael Cathedral, was almost reduced to rubble by German bombing on November 14 1940. It was decided to leave the 14th-century cathedral in ruins as a memorial to the suffering of all people during World War Two. Some of the walls have been restored, but the old cathedral is just a roofless shell, with a fire-blackened "charred Cross" at the place of the altar. This was made from roof beams which fell during the bombing. Lady Epstein has donated Jacob's *Ecce Homo*, 1935, to this church and it has been placed along the inner wall. The people decided to build a new, modern church right next to the old cathedral, and artists from all over the world were commissioned to do art for it. My brother's *St. Michael and the Devil* is so impressive. People come up and say: "Ohhh..." And then they take pictures. My brother never saw the finished church; it was dedicated in 1962.

In 1974 Marthe Clamage and her son Daniel stopped to see the Coventry Cathedrals during a visit to England after a summer which Marthe spent teaching in an exchange program in Valenciennes, France. She and Daniel were admiring her uncle's *Michael*, which was posed for by Wynne Godley, Jacob's daughter Kitty's second husband. A young cleric came by and Marthe decided to ask him why Epstein's work was put on the outside, when Eric Gill and everybody else is inside, you know.

"Oh," said the young man, "it's because Epstein was a Jew, you know. Our Board of Trustees didn't want a Jew in the Cathedral."

Daniel said to him: "Do you know who this woman is?

The young man said no. Daniel said: "She's Sir Jacob Epstein's niece." The man got very upset and started to apologize to Marthe.

Marthe said: "Don't apologize. They unintentionally gave him the best place of all." She's right. Jacob has the place of honor.

* * * * * *

Jacob died on the Jewish Day of *L'Chaim*, Life, in 1959. He had a heart attack. My husband would not let me go to the funeral. They had a very big, state funeral, but the rabbi wouldn't officiate because Epstein was to be buried in unhallowed ground – the Putney Vale Cemetery outside of London. Lady Kathleen chose it because of its natural countryside. Since no orthodox rabbi will officiate at an interment in unhallowed ground, Jacob's old friend, the Archbishop of Canterbury, conducted the service.

---

*The cathedral dates from the 11th Century, and is a mixed style, early Gothic-Romanesque.

I don't know what Jacob felt about his burial services; he never indicated anything to me about what he wanted. I do know that one of the executors of his estate, a Jew, was very mad because he was not buried as a Jew. Jewish sevices for the dead are very simple. The dead are wrapped in winding sheets, like Epstein's first *Christ* and his *Lazarus,* and they are buried before sundown of the following day.

In 1966 Lady Epstein and Sally Fortune Ryan gave the plaster model for the Llandaff *Majestas* to the Riverside Church in New York City. The Llandaff parishioners were very upset about this. They understood that they were to have the only one. It was a special commission and Jacob had designed it for Llandaff. Although the people in Wales tried to stop the gift to Riverside, they were not able to do it. The *Majestas* plaster model is placed in back of the Riverside Church pipe organ. It is up very high above the organ, suspended in the second balcony over the entrance to the nave. The model has been gilded and it is lighted with spotlights. The interior of the nave is very dark.

My niece, Florence Solomon, Chana's daughter, and I went to Europe in 1973 and we saw the beautiful Coventry Cathedrals. Lady Epstein was in Italy, at her villa on Lake Garda. Although she had hoped to come back and meet us, she was unable to do so. Lady Kathleen died in 1979.*

After Jacob's death his African art collection was sold and parts of it have entered other famous art collectors' holdings. The late Nelson Rockefeller acquired some pieces which my brother owned.** During his lifetime Jacob would never part with any of it. He truly loved art and all his life was dedicated to it.

I bet you think the story is over. Well, we did too when we began this book. One day in 1977, Marthe and I went to visit my brother, Dr. Irving Epstein. Marthe and I started to talk about my brother Hyman. I was so young when he died; I never knew much about him or what happened. Irving told us that Hymie was around seventeen years old in 1899 and he got into trouble with some of his Irish friends. You see, Hymie was an athlete, a very vigorous young man, and he had a lot of Irish friends on the Lower East Side. My brother Jacob remarked about this in his *Autobiography* and said that Hyman had a scrappy personality. Hymie got into trouble with his friends and he was arrested and imprisoned on Ward's Island. Irving said he knew this because he was sent on Saturdays to give Hymie the food his mother had prepared. I remember going there with my mother too, and bringing food, but I never knew where I was. They never told me anything at all about it. Irving said that mother was pregnant with Harold when Hymie was put into prison. While Hymie was in prison he started studying Catholicism. Irving said he converted to Catholicism, but we are not sure about this because Hymie is buried in a Jewish cemetery. There were a lot of Irish in prison and of course the priests used to come around all the time. My father tried to get Hymie pardoned. He appealed to Governor Odell* but the governor would do nothing. Hymie tried to escape. He swam the East River but he got caught in a whirlpool and was captured. Hymie was in prison the rest of his life. He died at twenty-seven years of age on May 29, 1909.

Oh, Hymie was beautiful, a *beautiful* young man with an athletic build. He had bright red hair curling down to his ears and blue eyes. He looked like the rest of us, like Mary Epstein, but he was the most handsome of all – a Greek god.

---

*Lady Kathleen and Sylvia Press never met, nor did Sylvia ever meet any of Lady Kathleen's children. Lady Epstein and Sylvia corresponded, primarily on business relating to Mrs. Press's purchase of the *Nehru.* Lady Epstein tried to buy back the *Churchill* from Mrs. Press but she would not sell, so Mrs Press told me. Mrs. Press was also very annoyed because Lady Epstein had made further issues from Epstein's molds and had sold them.

**Nelson Rockefeller's collection of primitive art can be seen in the Michael C. Rockefeller Wing of the Metropolitan Museum of Art, New York City. *Smithsonian Magazine,* February, 1982, page 41, reproduced an illustration of a Fang reliquary head which had been in Epstein's collection; see article by Charlotte Moser.

*Governor Benjamin B. Odell, Jr., 1901-1905.

After Irving told us he became very upset because he had promised never to tell about it. All pictures of Hyman Epstein were destroyed after his death, as far as we know. He was never discussed except as a bad boy who had converted to Catholicism. We younger children, Harold and I, never knew anything. I was not told the story until 1977 and Harold died without knowing it. Irving did not tell us what it was that Hymie did which caused him to be imprisoned, but it must have been minor, for the prisons around New York City then were workhouses, and he was probably in the reformatory because of his age.

My brother, Dr. Irving Epstein, died at the age of eighty-six on January 28, 1979.

Plate 49: *Lucifer* (detail)

Plate 50: *Lucifer* (side view)

Plate 52: *The Bowater House Group*

Plate 53: *Time,* from *Social Consciousness*

Plate 54: *The Rock Drill*

Plate 55: Sylvia Epstein Press, 1976

Plate 56: *Lucifer* (detail)

Plate 57: *Majestas* (detail), Photographs by S. Travers, AIBP, by Permission of the Dean and Chapter of Llandaff Cathedral

Plate 58: *New York Madonna & Child* (detail)

Plate 59: *The Sun God* (obverse), The Metropolitan Museum of Art, New York City, Gift of Kathleen Epstein and Sally Ryan in Memory of Jacob Epstein, 1970, (Epstein, stone, 1910)

Plate 60: *Primeval Gods* (reverse) The Metropolitan Museum of Art, New York City, Gift of Kathleen Epstein and Sally Ryan in Memory of Jacob Epstein, 1970, (Epstein, Stone, 1933)

A POSTSCRIPT by Jane F. Babson

The visit by Mrs. Press and Mrs Clamage to Dr. Irving Epstein's home at which time the story of Hyman Epstein was told occurred during the week when I visited the Davis and Long Gallery in New York City. While I was studying *The Sunflower* and *The Rock Drill* I said to myself, "It (the theme) is Mary Epstein and Hyman." The next day, while walking down the street, a voice within me told me to go and look at the photographs of the *Oscar Wilde Tomb*. I did so and the connection was completed.

Excitedly I called Mrs. Clamage after the discovery and told her that I thought I knew what Hyman had done. "Worse than that", she said. "He was in prison – the greatest disgrace for a Jewish family." She then told me the story of the visit and later added details which Mrs. Press had forgotten when she and I discussed the story. According to Marthe, Dr. Irving Epstein was sent to identify the body after Hyman had died. She also told me that when she and her aunt went to Washington Cemetery and looked up the Epstein burial records they were directed to a burial plot for Hyman which contained only two graves. Both headstones were so eroded by the weather that it was not possible to determine which grave was Hyman Epstein's.

City, court and prison documents of this period in New York City are very incomplete. During the writing of this book, an old warehouse was opened near the East Side piers in New York City. Stacked on the floor were city records dating from the middle of the nineteenth century but in most cases they were indecipherable and many had been destroyed by lack of care.

Throughout my research for this book extraordinary things happened as I traced the unknown theme of Epstein's work. Walt Whitman's *Leaves of Grass* fell open at pages where poems directly related to the theme could be found. Events occurred which were related to Epstein's themes and I had astonishing dreams. The most extraordinary experiences occurred on my trip abroad to photograph the Epstein sculpture. A major connection fell into place in the deserts of Syria. This discovery will be described in the following pages.

AN APPRECIATION OF SOME OF THE ART OF SIR JACOB EPSTEIN

Art is the distillation of the artist's personal reality. He draws upon all his conscious and unconscious imagery and experience. The work of art is a composite of many different things; what is seen and remarked upon and what is felt through emotion and refined through experience. It includes both contemporary and past events. The artist goes deeply into the well of his mind, as has been described by Mark Twain. He transmutes, and, at times, transforms, his experiences, especially those of deep feeling, psychological pain, and shame, or guilt. These sources often appear in his work as veiled symbols; the artist himself may not recognize them for what they are.

The artist always deals with themes which interest him intellectually. He takes certain ideas and pushes them through various stages of development until he reaches his personal conclusion. His family, himself, his education (intellectual, religious and artistic), and his tastes – they are all present in a true work of art. When this art touches universal or common experience, it may be said that it is art in its finest development. Among the ideas which interest artists are the study of form, which includes both realistic and abstract shapes, landscape, light, and people's appearances. Sir Jacob Epstein was interested in developing all aspects of sculpture, technically and artistically, to portray psychological states of mind. He wanted to be like Donatello, the great psychological artist of the Renaissance. Epstein admired the extraordinary achievements of the artists of the Renaissance; this is an important fact which should be kept constantly in mind while studying his work. It is also necessary to know the personal life and the facts of the family background of Sir Jacob Epstein in order to understand the themes of his great monumental sculpture. Through the American family members, in particular the memoirs of Mrs. Sylvia Press, the words of his first wife Margaret, a study of his monumental art, Epstein's own words and the literature he read, I have been given an intimate look into the mind of a great artist of the Twentieth Century. This, of course, is not all there is to know about the art of Epstein. Every great work of art and every good artist must be studied from many points of view. I have not attempted to study the Celtic sources, the influence of African art, the other English artists who frequented the Café Royal, etc., but the American family background is an aspect of Epstein's development which has been falsified and ignored until now. It has been a most serious oversight on the part of historians, who too readily have accepted myths about Epstein, i.e., that his family in America were poor and of peasant stock. Through specially selected family and art photographs, included with this study, it will become apparent how important Sir Jacob's American family was to his development of his art, and also how important Epstein's monumental art really is to an understanding of our age, which has, until now, been defined purely by the Abstract Movement.

In 1899 the Epstein family moved away from Hester Street and up to 1661 Madison Avenue in New York City. Although we were originally led to believe that the reason for the move was to enable the Epsteins to leave Hester Street for a more fashionable neighborhood, it is now obvious that this may have been only part of the reason. The disgrace of their son Hyman's imprisonment must have been a motivating factor. Considering the strict, moralistic tone of American society at that time, one can only imagine that deep pain which this tragedy inflicted upon all of the family members. This, plus the frequent ridicule by his father, probably explains why the young Jacob refused to live with his family uptown, and why he spent so much time at the courts downtown. Jacob Epstein was a sensitive, idealistic and moral young man. His brother Hyman was a dear companion, and by all accounts a fine young man. The heartbreak that this event inflicted upon a man like Jacob Epstein created deep psychological pain, but, as is true of so much artistic experience, it also gave him one of his great themes – Beauty – The Evil Eye. God of the Sun.

Jacob left his home in 1902 for study in Paris. The obvious reasons Epstein left America have been written about for years, but it seems obvious now that the primary reason was not anti-Semitism. This was the reason I was given during my formal art education, and it has intrigued me for many years. Why, if the reason was purely because Jacob was a Jew, would he have gone to Paris or London to live? Surely the anti-Semitism which was slowly developing at this time in Europe and was to culminate in the atrocities of World War Two, would have offered even less opportunity to a man so hypersensitive as to flee a land he loved dearly. It was the obvious falsity of this reason which led me to explore the possibility that art historians, as usual, were too quick to ascribe superficial qualities to artists' motivations.

I believe there is also a direct correlation between the young Jacob Epstein and Hutchins Hapgood's description of the young Jewish man in 1902. This can be found in Hapgood's *The Spirit of the Ghetto*, where the author first describes the young Jew as dual in personality in regarding his culture. On the one hand he sees the great material opportunities which assimilation into American culture will offer him. On the other hand he longs for the closed-in serenity which he sees in the life of orthodoxy practiced by his immigrant parents; in particular the life of his father. It seems to me that Epstein must have been influenced deeply by this book which offered him his first professional commission. Although his illustrations are only the first indications of what he was capable of doing, they are also the first synthesis of his themes. The themes of exotica, intellectualism, and variety of human types which were developed by Hapgood and illustrated by Epstein, lead directly into his first real sculptural commission, the *Four Stages of Life*, 1907, British Medical Association Building in the Strand, London. The photographs which I have seen of Epstein's work executed at the Ecole des Beaux-Arts, around 1902, in which young, Rodinesque women and sensitive young men are portrayed in a most accomplished, graceful way, further document the growth of this theme, Life, which was to occupy the artist all his life. The dualism continues as his work splits into two parts, his monumental sculpture and his portraits, the latter done to earn a living. Epstein's duality is also illustrated in his personal life. How much of this is conscious will never be known, but the Biblical allusions and overtones of Jacob (Israel), the founder of the Hebrew tribal society, must not be overlooked by anyone interested in the artistic, familial, and literary synthesis of Epstein's art. A study should also be made of the story of the Egyptian goddess Isis, Osiris's sister and wife, who resurrected him from the dead after his destruction by his brother, Set, who had red hair. Isis's salvation of Amon-Ra's immortality by her use of the bite of a poisonous snake to wrest the secret name from the sun god should also not be ignored. Attention should also be paid to the fact that the cult of Osiris, with his resurrection by Isis, replaced in Egypt the cult of Amon-Ra as the great god of the underworld and of light – eternal life.

Jacob Epstein's love of children and his portrayals of them for pleasure directly parallel the interest of the Italian Renaissance artists in the *putti*. In Epstein's case, I believe that his children's portraits provided bridges from his temporal or materialistic concerns with portraits, to his great artistic work, the monumental sculpture.

Life on the Lower East Side in New York was rich, sensual, and exciting. Great social and artistic movements were born in the cafés and houses on Hester Street. Epstein never forgot the stimulus of those years; he told his niece Marthe that he looked back on America with great nostalgia. One of the poets whose work he greatly admired and studied was Walt Whitman. From these sources Epstein developed his great, encompassing theme – the circle of life.

Epstein's marriage to Margaret Gilmour Dunlop occurred very soon after his return from

America in 1905. His attempts to reconcile his aspirations and relations with those of his family had failed. He was impoverished and the companionship and support which Margaret offered him may have replaced, in his mind, the help formerly given him by his mother and Chana. Margaret Epstein occupied an extraordinary place in Jacob's life. She became indispensable, and she must have provided unusual intellectual and emotional support. Members of the Epstein family have told me that Jacob was an intellectual and that if he had not become an artist he would have undoubtedly been a writer or an academician. It is possible that Margaret introduced Epstein to the great English literature of Calvinism and encouraged him in developing this aspect of his themes, for she was a writer herself. The great *Lazarus*, 1947, was executed the year of Margaret Epstein's death. It bears a reworked portrait of the first bust of Margaret Epstein, 1905. It appears to be a combination of this early portrait and quite possibly a death mask study. This explains why the head sits so awkwardly on the body, enclosed in a winding sheet. The work was bought by New College, Oxford, a fact which delighted Epstein, and possibly indicates recognition of Margaret's intellectual support. The dualism in this work is apparent if one reads the story of Lazarus in the New Testament. There are two stories of Lazarus; one is the obvious one of Lazarus raised by Christ from the dead (see St. John, 11, 41:46), and the other, the Lazarus story of the man who was a beggar, covered with sores, who sat and begged at the city gates. He was ignored by the rich man who passed by until after both had died. The rich man, burning in hell, looked up to heaven and saw Lazarus in the bosom of Abraham and begged that Lazarus would cool his forehead with water. Abraham refused to allow it (see St. Luke, 16, 18:31).

The Jewish artistic tradition is humanistic and realistic in form. Epstein's work from early beginnings was developed in humanistic and realistic expressionism. It is surprising to see the appearance in 1910 of his first abstract work, *The Sunflower*, unless one is aware of the tragic death of Hyman Epstein in 1909. Shortly after Hymie's death, Epstein's work becomes increasingly dual in concept and abstract in form. The great theme of life begins to split. One cannot discount the influence of the other art movements in Europe, particularly in Paris, at this time. Abstractionism, based on African, Egyptian, and primitive forms, was developing. Picasso's overall view of the human form was evolving from Egyptian painting and African art, as well as from his personal experiences. Epstein knew Picasso and all the artists of Montmartre. Epstein was also researching his work for the new Oscar Wilde Tomb commission, in the British Museum and the Louvre in Paris. This research continued all his life, by his own admission. At this time Epstein is searching also for a style, although he is now technically proficient.

The Sunflower and *The Sun God*, (whose reverse side, dated 1933, portrays *Primeval Gods*) both appear in 1910. *The Sun God* is not finished until 1933. In 1909 the death of Hymie coincides with the receipt of the Oscar Wilde Tomb commission. *The Sunflower* carries the first portrayal of the mask of the Epstein face. It is also the first manifestation of Amon-Ra, but the face is that of Mary Epstein and all the Epstein children resembled her. Since intermarriage was so common in Jewish families, as their choices were necessarily limited by the restrictions of the European *shtetl*, it is possible that Max, whose real name was Chatskel Barntovsky, was a distant cousin to Mary Solomon, for genealogically the Barnato, Isaacs and Salomon families are related. Names were adapted and changed to fit the circumstances. If this possibility is true, it explains the extraordinary facial similarities of all of the children. *The Sun God* is the first attempt by Epstein to portray the physical beauty and athletic grace of the Epsteins, in particular that of Hyman.

Jacob's studies in the Louvre and the British Museum undoubtedly took his research into the Middle East, to the Egyptian sculptures and tomb paintings, and to the art of the Orient. This study would include, beside that of the Far East, Assyro-Babylonian, Persian, Greek, Hittite, Rome in the Orient, and the later mixed Christian-Semitic art of Syria. Palmyra, Syria, is an ancient oasis where oriental camel caravans loaded with trade stopped on their way into what is now Israel. At the Temple of Bel in Palmyra there is a large stone bas-relief of a young moon god, believed to date from the Second or Third Century A.D. In the museum in Palmyra there are other bas-reliefs of both the sun and moon gods; the representation is almost the same in each case. The young man is dressed in a linear, toga-like garment and his curly hair is arranged in a circular, ray-like halo. The military gods are also aspects of the sun god. In the Egyptian *Book of the Dead*, the sun and moon are believed to be the eyes of Amon-Ra, the great god of creation. In ancient style Amon-Ra is represented by a stone obelisk; in mythology he kept his eyes closed to preserve his lustre. He daily rode his sun-boat across the sky of the world and went underground in his moon-boat at night to reappear as the dawn. This myth is later fused into that of Helios, the great Greek god of the sun, of which Apollo, god of manly beauty and giver of plagues, is one aspect.

Jacob Epstein developed the Epstein face as a mask for the flying demon angel which he carved for the memorial to Oscar Wilde. Epstein himself calls this figure a demon angel and says that he researched it for a long period. The similarities between the treatment of the art of Wilde and that of his art must have appeared shockingly apt to the young Epstein, for both were maligned and ridiculed. One of the symbols used to ridicule Wilde in the American press after his speaking tour of the United States was the sunflower. Wilde, dressed in velvet knee pants, is portrayed as holding one in his hand. Wilde's imprisonment, subsequent ruination by gossip and slander, injustice in the courts, and conversion to Catholicism paralleled Epstein's brother Hyman's experience. Oscar Wilde also wrote two great poems, *The Ballad of Reading Gaol* and *The Sphinx*, both of which were undoubtedly part of the basis for the tomb's concept. The great Sphinx of Giza is believed to be the personification of Amon-Ra, with astrological connotations, and the answer to the well-known riddle of the sphinx is, of course, *Man.*

Epstein, however, was no illustrator. He was an artist and his research took him into many areas in searching for the Wilde Tomb's concept. There are two major Nineteenth-Century tomb monuments in America which are familiar to all students of art history. When Epstein was a young student of George Grey Barnard's at the New York Art Students League, these two monuments were relatively new, still creating interest among aspiring artists. The first work is *The Jacob Bigelow Sphinx*, executed in 1872 by Martin Milmore. It is a memorial to a young man and the young sculptor had been his friend. Milmore's own memorial, the famous *Death Staying the Hand of the Sculptor*, was later executed by Daniel Chester French. The Bigelow Sphinx is in Mount Auburn Cemetery in Cambridge, Massachusetts. The form is that of a recumbent sphinx and it is carved in granite. The face of the sphinx is that of a young man, possibly an idealized likeness of the deceased. On one side of the base is carved a Latin inscription, the translation of which is included on the opposite side. It is a memorial to the dead of the Civil War. This form is very like that utilized by Epstein in Oscar Wilde's Tomb and the later work, *Social Consciousness*, 1954, Philadelphia. It should also be remarked that Mount Auburn Cemetery, first opened in 1831, is famous for its important historical personages's graves. It contains monuments executed by artists such as Augustus Saint-Gaudens and Thomas Crawford. Near the Bigelow Sphinx is a small church called the Bigelow Chapel. It contains a crematorium and has some of the architectural qualities of *La Sainte-Chapelle* in Paris, particularly in its stained glass windows. Mount Auburn is planted, like *Père Lachaise*, with flowers and large avenues of trees, and it was apparently intended by our Victorian citizens to be a necropolis, or city of the dead.

The other famous American tomb which Epstein undoubtedly studied was *The Adams Memorial* by Augustus Saint-Gaudens, 1891, in Rock Creek Cemetery in Washington, D.C. The architectural setting for the tomb was designed by Stanford White. The memorial was erected by Henry Adams to his wife, Marion Hooper Adams, who died a suicide in 1885. Henry Adams is also buried there. Mrs. Adams was a very intellectual and gifted woman, but the identity of the shrouded, seated woman of the tomb is unknown. The material of the sculpture is bronze; the soft green patina blends beautifully with the shrubs and trees. It was said that Eleanor Roosevelt often visited this tomb while living in Washington. The site is quiet and beautiful, and the female form, popularly called *Grief,* is one of the finest works of Saint-Gaudens. Various meanings have been placed upon the figure, according to the literature supplied by Rock Creek Cemetery. Among the interpretations are *Infinite Wisdom* (John Hay) and *The Peace of God.* (Saint Gaudens). Saint-Gaudens also attributed the source of its conception to oriental thought, according to his son, Homer Saint-Gaudens.

The combination of the form of *The Bigelow Sphinx* and the mystery of the female figure of *The Adams Memorial* must have influenced Epstein's concept for the Wilde Tomb. The Oscar Wilde Tomb in *Père Lachaise* became a double tomb, a secret memorial to his brother, Hyman Epstein. Although Epstein never knew Wilde (Wilde died in 1900 in Paris), Sir Jacob Epstein made a trip to *Père Lachaise* with his second wife in 1955 and laid sunflowers before the Wilde Tomb[1].

Although the symbolism of the Oscar Wilde Tomb must, of course, be developed in relation to Wilde, the deciphering of it in this book will relate to the secret symbolism and concept of Jacob Epstein's memorial to his brother. The Seven Deadly Sins, which appear so puzzling, relate to those of the Bible (see Proverbs, 6, 16-19). They are described as *pride, falsehood, homicide, calumny, mischief, perjury* and *discord among men.* There are also the Seven Deadly Sins of Dante's Inferno, which correspond to the Nine Circles of Hell, i.e., variations of the Biblical sins, such as *lust, bestiality, avarice, fraud,* ending in the greatest of all sins, *treason.* Lucifer, the great betrayer of God, is in the lowest circle of ice, for his is the greatest of sins. One must also keep in mind the Kabbalists' mystic philosophy, for Jacob Epstein was of orthodox background. The demonology which is found in both the Kabbalah and orthodox Judaism corresponds to these Seven Sins found on the crown of the flying angel. The crown, in Kabbalistic symbolism, represents the intellect, or head of man, the divine manifestation of God. God, in Judaism, is one, divine wisdom, and in the Kabbalah, God, the Ancient of Ancients, has only one face – the faces of Man.

In orthodox Jewish families, particularly those of the immigrants of the Lower East Side, children were often given a Jewish name and a common, or secular name. This practice is common to many peoples and the belief in the power of a secret name is also found in the legend of the Sun God, Amon-Ra, whose secret name kept him safe from the attempts of the devil, Āapep, who daily tried to destroy him as he rode in his sun boat across the sky. The Kabbalists believed in many names for God, using numbers which corresponded to the letters of the Hebrew alphabet to combine for names of God. The secret name and identity attached by Jacob Epstein to the Oscar Wilde Tomb must have appealed to his sense of ironic justice, for Hyman, also Herman and Hyam, in the Hebrew *Chaim,* means "Life".

Art Deco motifs can also be seen in the flying wings of the demon angel of the Wilde Tomb, but the disturbing element is the continuation of the immobility of the form, first seen in 1910. This immobility apparently indicates great inner stress in Epstein and continues to surface periodically in his work until after World War Two. It should be recalled that Mary Epstein died in 1913. The immobility continues in the realistic work of the *Risen Christ,* 1919, *Ecce Homo,* 1935, *Consummation Est,* 1936, and reappears again in *Lazarus,* 1947.

1913 appears to have been a decisive year for Epstein[2]. During this year he also begins work on his completely abstract *Rock Drill,* which went through several stages and was completed in 1915. In

---

1 See Buckle, Richard, *Jacob Epstein, Sculptor,* Faber and Faber, Ltd., London, 1963, page 63.

2 In January, 1978, Marthe Clamage visited Mexico City and while there saw the Diego Rivera Retrospective in the Palace of Fine Arts. She identified an unknown painting in the exhibition, *El Escultor,* 1913 (lent anonymously) as a portrait of her uncle, Sir Jacob Epstein. The painting shows Epstein seated in a blue demin coat and he holds a stylized Egyptian mask in his hand. One wonders if Rivera may have participated in the 1913 raid on the Wilde sculpture by artists, who ripped off the metal shield put over the penis of the angel. Rivera had been exiled from Mexico; Epstein knew Rivera in Paris.

1913 Jacob Epstein helped found the London Group, whose purpose ostensibly was to make clean, basic and pure forms. All the outward manifestations of the motives of this group have been explored elsewhere. I am here concerned with the psychologically disturbing aspect of the *Rock Drill.* On page 45 of *The Sculptor Speaks,* Epstein remarks that the *Rock Drill* referred to an incident which happened in New York; the obvious interpretation will be the spectacle of a man operating a pneumatic drill, and the dehumanization, the shaking and immobility of man's torso in the occupation. This is, of course, part of the concept, but one must see the actual bronze to be fully aware of the hidden concept. The puzzling visor-head on its swivel neck is not that of the masked pneumatic drill operator. Neither is it a derivation, at least not directly, of Epstein in his *Self Portrait,* 1912, where he is shown in a cap. This work is done directly from a photograph of Epstein. The mask on the *Rock Drill* is a direct rendition of the Greek armor helmet. As I looked at it, I heard Sylvia Press saying: "Beautiful, beautiful, like a Greek god," and I saw that this symbol is another manifestation of the sun god – Hyman Epstein – the wandering demon-angel of the Wilde Tomb. This is further borne out by contemporary sketches for the *Rock Drill* which show a helmeted, flying figure. Life here is frozen; the child in the armor of the torso is a still-born fetus. Life is alienation, and death. The Great Mother is dead.

Epstein considered war an abomination; this is most decisively expressed in his *T.U.C. War Memorial,* 1957. The great snake monster holds the limp body of Man in its hands; this monster is both War and the Great Mother synthesized in horror. In 1913 World War One was about to erupt. Epstein remarks in *The Sculptor Speaks,* on the page previously mentioned, that the *Rock Drill* is not entirely abstract, for it deals with World War One. It is understandable that Margaret Epstein would become quite alarmed over the direction Epstein's art had taken. Shaken by the vilification which he endured in the police action taken on his Wilde Tomb, and most surely deeply saddened by the deaths of his brother, mother, and friends in this period, i.e., the Great War, Epstein sought expression via abstraction. The Epsteins were also in desperate need of money and at this time had been taken under the patronage of John Quinn. Quinn was a master manipulator of the art world and its artists. He played the artists he favored and collected in the way that Wall Street brokers juggled stocks; Quinn offered financial support and sales in America. Epstein was an American and he recognized the game, which ended when Quinn, tiring of Epstein's complaints about Quinn's profiteering, sold him short just before Quinn's death in 1924[3].

Margaret Epstein knew that Jacob must be allowed to externalize his great inner torment through art. She and Jacob wrote a series of letters to Quinn, imploring him to do what he could to keep Epstein from being drafted into the British Army.[4] Quinn did make efforts, but at the same time wrote them chauvinistic letters, shaming Jacob Epstein for his lack of patriotism. Quinn was blatantly anti-German, anti-Semitic, and anti-Irish, although of Irish stock himself. Jacob Epstein was drafted in 1917 and in 1918 he was invalided out of the army, after suffering a complete nervous breakdown. He wrote Quinn on July 20, 1918, and told him of this, mentioned that for five months he was not allowed to see mail, and remarked that he wished to continue his favorite work, monumental art[5].

It appears that after 1918 Epstein clarified his style and renewed the development of his great theme – Life. The model Sunita, her sister, and Sunita's son, Enver, entered his home shortly after Epstein met them in 1924. These three people introduced new physical types to Epstein – the exotica and mysticism of the Orient. It also seems likely that Epstein's readings in the poetry of Walt Whitman, religion, Hudson's *Green Mansions,* Milton's *Paradise Lost,* and art history were creating new aesthetic images.

---

3 See Reid, B.L. *The Man from New York, John Quinn and His Friends,* Oxford University Press, New York, page 616.
4 Ibid, page 258.
5 Ibid, page 374.

In 1925 *The Hudson Memorial* was unveiled in Hyde Park, London. It is placed in the center of a bird sanctuary, surrounded by trees and shrubs. This monument was the result of a commission Jacob Epstein had received to create a memorial to the English author-naturalist, W.H. Hudson. Hudson's book, *Green Mansions,* combined artistic imagery, naturalism and theosophy. The book had been very well received and the furore created by the public over the female figure of Rima, the bird goddess, was an unexpected shock to the artist. He later dubbed this reaction to his work as "Rimaphobia" and used the term often in speaking of art in *The Sculptor Speaks.*

The figure of Rima, angularly carved, is a combined European-Oriental type. The composition of the sculpture is directly traceable to *The Ludovisi Throne,* a transitional Greek sculpture now in the National Museum of the Terme, Rome. *The Ludovisi Throne* is now believed to show a woman in the squatting position of childbirth, in the act of creation. The male in *Green Mansions* is Abel, the artist-traveller, who discovers the burned bones and ashes of Rima after she has fallen into the burning tree and has been destroyed by savage tribes who do not understand who she is. Abel carries the bones of Rima with him for the rest of his life. Another companion who goes with Abel through life is the snake monster, always watching and always visible at the edge of the dark. The identification of Epstein with Abel and Rima, the pure artist and artistic ideal, should now be clear. Outwardly calm when attacked by the press and public, Epstein inwardly suffered great distress. Rima, with all its connotations, echoed the attacks on the Wilde Tomb in 1913. It reinforced his bitterness towards the public's response to his art.

The lovely work, *The Visitation,* appears in 1926. Here the young virgin awaits God – the Annunciation. This is a theme straight out of the Italian Renaissance, but it is reworked by Epstein's own experience. The girl is about eleven years old and her hands are folded in humility. The face is that of Sylvia Epstein, the beloved little sister with the long golden hair, arranged in the pigtails of the little girls of the Lower East Side. Epstein had not seen Sylvia since 1905 when she was about ten years old. This rendition of a family member as the Virgin is not a new one; it was commonly employed by both Italian and German artists during the Renaissance.

The next year, 1927, Epstein executed *The New York Madonna,* which was posed for by Sunita and her son Enver. The oriental quality of passive acceptance and contemplation makes this work extraordinary. Another remarkable quality about the model Sunita is that her face is an almost exact duplication of the features of all the Epsteins. Sunita became one of Epstein's favorite models, in particular for his monumental work. The theme within a theme appealed to his intellectualism. Sunita became the mask for the duality of his monuments dealing with the sun god, Hyman Epstein. The only subtle difference in Epstein's rendering of Sunita's face and that of the monumental art is the treatment of the area below the eye sockets. Sunita's face lacked the bony protuberance of the skull below the eye sockets. This protuberance is clearly visible in *The Visitation, Israfel, Lucifer, Majestas* in Llandaff, and the Great Mother of the *Social Conciousness.* It is very evident in Mrs. Press's photographic portrait, taken by me in 1976. One should also compare the similarities in Epstein, Sylvia, and Irving, in the group snapshot taken at Long Beach, New York, in 1954, during Epstein's final visit to America. Epstein's private joke, his private theme, begins to appear around 1926, and develops over the following years into essential and universal forms of expression.

From 1924 on, preliminary studies of the great themes begin to appear in Epstein's art – the *Seraph,* 1924, which bears an idealized version of the Epstein face, as does the unfinished *Angel of the Annunciation.* These images from *Paradise Lost* and Christian and Jewish religion will continue all of Epstein's creative life. *The First Portrait of Kathleen,* ca. 1921, is Epstein's second wife as she first appeared to him. The beautiful, young and innocent girl forecasts the circle of *Genesis,* 1930, and the young Madonna holding the Christ in Social Consciousness.

In 1927 Margaret Epstein arranged a trip to America for her family, in hopes of obtaining new commissions for Jacob and re-establishing Epstein in America. The trip was abortive for several reasons. The fact that Americans at cocktail parties in New York looked at Epstein as if he were a curious freak must have intensified his sense of alienation in his native country. The lack of any American museum capable of providing the research opportunities available to him at the British Museum indicated that he could not continue his research into essential elements of art and life in America. Margaret's self-delusion in regard to her attempts to estrange Epstein from his second family are sadly obvious in her letters. Epstein returned to England and his second rupture with his American relatives was not healed until after World War Two.

The great *Day* and *Night* sculptures for the London Underground Headquarters were executed in 1929. The Epstein face, here a violent version of the *Sun God*, appears on the great father *Day*; the model for the little boy placed in an Egyptian stance, facing his father, was Theodore Garman. In this version the Epstein face bears some of the qualities of the later snake monster. The *Night* sculpture, which also carries traces of the snake in its face, depicts the Great Mother holding the limp body of Man as he sleeps. Echoes of Michaelangelo's *Night* and *Day* sculptures from the Medici Chapel in Florence are present, as is the composition of Michaelangelo's *Pietà*, St. Peter's, Rome. However, literary images also occur in these works. *Paradise Lost*, Book Eleven, and *The Kabbalah* both describe metaphysical states. In the Kabbalistic reference, the soul is described as ascending to God while Man sleeps. Man's body then becomes limp, drained of vital spirits and animated only by a breath of life which comes from his heart.[6]

Israfel, 1931, is a curious but seminal work. Sunita is the masking model; her epicene qualities are emphasized here. She has the long, curly hair of the *Sun God* and the later works, and the bust is masculine. The name of the piece is a combination of letters, a Kabbalistic riddle. The title is a combination of *Israel, Lucifer,* and *Michael,* and it is a prophecy of later works.

The use and support of a stronger soul to carry the weaker one through transmigration is a Kabbalistic thesis[7]. It is difficult to see here which is the stronger of the two Epsteins – Hyman or Jacob. The Epstein face here is hollow-eyed and alienated, a mask. The ultimate triumph through the Archangel Michael is forecast, however. The combination of the letters of the names of the three personalities – Israel (Jacob), Lucifer (Devil-Evil), and Michael (Triumph and Assumption) – spell out a secret reference to God, the Beginning and the End.

The early *Sun God*, which was first begun in 1910, was completed by Epstein in 1933, one year after the great archaeological finds at Dura Europos in Syria. This city, which is located on the ancient route to Iraq, contained a synagogue contemporary with the Roman occupation. When this ruin was excavated, monumental Jewish frescoes were revealed[8]. They are painted in the heroic Pompeiian style and the composition on the wall is developed as an orderly procession of the great Jewish religious figures from the *Torah*. The mixed Roman-Orientalism was also revealed in another site at Dura Europos, the Temple of Bel, ca. 239 A.D. A fragment from the frescoes there is now in the Yale University Art Gallery in New Haven, Conn. Sun and moon gods are portrayed in this work, entitled *The Sacrifice of Julius Terentius to the Palmyrene Gods*, and one sees the same style of painting in these works as in the Roman frescoes at Pompeii. These great archaeological finds must have spurred Epstein's efforts to finish the concept of *The Sun God* of 1910, and probably seemed justification for his belief that he was the artistic interpreter of the Judeo-Christian cultures.

In 1933 von Hindenburg appointed Adolf Hitler as Reich Chancellor in Germany, and the first concentration camp, Dachau, was built. The Burning of the Books occurred on May 10th of that year. In 1934 Hitler became Head of State and Commander of the German Army. The nightmare is to begin again; the serpent, Satan, is again stalking the world. The frozen, accusatory *Risen Christ,*

6 Francke, Adolph, *The Kabbalah, The Religious Philosophy of the Hebrews,* Bell Publishing Company, New York, 1960, page 126.
7 *Ibid,* pp. 133-134.
8 The original frescoes are now in The National Museum, Damascus, Syria.

1919, reappears in Epstein's *Ecce Homo*, 1935. The Epstein face has become the face of Christ, the earthly representation of God, the celestial and second Adam, described in the *Kabbalah* and *Paradise Lost*. This God of Light is now in chains. The horror of war will be much worse, the sculpture seems to say. The War in heaven, led by Satan and his legions with their infernal machines, is about to begin.

For all of us who lived through World War Two, the stone memorial of the Epstein *Ecce Homo*, now placed in the ruined St. Michael's Cathedral in Coventry, is a deeply moving evocation of that dreadful time. Executed in the midst of the suffering of those years, it is a more successful memorial to the millions of dead than the self-conscious art contained within the new cathedral, a place which excluded Jacob Epstein because he was a Jew.

In the midst of those hellish days of World War Two, Epstein carved a single, white gardenia. Although it appeared mystifying to his public, this flower is described in *Green Mansions* as a strange, exotic flower,[9] appearing artificial in the light, discovered and admired by the artist-traveller, Abel. This flower exemplifies beauty, the Rima ideal. The gardenia motif was used by Espstein in his last *Portrait of Esther*, 1949, and his *Girl with Gardenias*, 1941, which is a portrait of Kathleen, middle-aged but still carrying a lovely, youthful body. The *Girl with Gardenias* was a sculpture whose reception by the public greatly disappointed Epstein. It appears to be a transitional piece: Eve-Spring; the composition derives partly from Botticelli's Flora in his painting, *Spring*, Uffizi, Florence.

Lucifer, 1944, now in the City Museums and Art Gallery, Birmingham, England, is a masterpiece, a perfect blending of great beauty mixed with horror and corruption. The traitorous Sun God has just landed in the final Circle of Hell after his Fall from Heaven. Although this sculpture is described as having been conceived from images in the First Book of *Paradise Lost*, it is Epstein's final rendition of the sun god as the evil spirit – Satan – the damned soul. The dark side of Man is about to be reabsorbed into the Light of Divine Wisdom. The defeat of Satan by the Second or Celestial Adam, Christ the Prince of Light, is imminent.

The Epstein face here bears an extraordinarily intense expression. I have only seen such intensity rendered in one other piece of sculpture, also a bronze: that is the transitional Greek work in Delphi, Greece, *The Charioteer of Delphi*. Both works have the quality of musing over the forthcoming contest of will and strength.

The handsome young torso of Epstein's serpent-god, Lucifer, has not yet begun to decay and the sculpture bears the beautiful and fresh mask of the Devil. The frontal rendition of the torso is beautiful. It is somewhat of a shock to walk around to the back and discover the female buttocks and graceful, female back. The gold-patinaed bronze is lit with an overhead gold spotlight. The effect is quietly beautiful.

Reaction to Lucifer is quick and decisive. It is a work which can not be dismissed. While photographing it, I asked a middle-aged guard what the public's reaction was to it.

"Well," he said, "a lot of people come up to it, gasp, and then say: 'Oh, that's obscene'. But I don't see that – the human body isn't obscene. Not if it's done properly."

"The Devil is obscene," I said. He agreed, and when I asked him what group of people were most upset by this work, calling it obscene, he told me it was mostly young people, although a few middle-aged people also reacted to it in this manner.

Youth Advancing, 1949, shows again the young sun god-athlete in what I think was his original conception, the young, seventeen-year-old Hyman Epstein. It quite possibly carries the true likeness of Hyman on the face, although all pictures of the young man were destroyed, (as far as we know,) by the Epstein family. The *Liverpool Giant*, 1954, Lewis's Department Store, Liverpool, is a huge, exultant bronze. It is a triumphal expression of the break-through (the dawn) of the soul to God – to Light. Amon-Ra, riding his boat between the mountains of the East and West – the architectural motifs on the sides of the boat suggest the Egyptian hieroglyphics – has defeated Āapep, the snake

9 Hudson, W.H. *Green Mansions*, The Modern Library Edition, Random House, New York, 1945, page 189.

devil, and appears in his true form, after his voyage through the underground regions. Here, also, I think that the form of the great god, the Greek Helios/Amon-Ra, is the true likeness of Hyman Epstein and that the face of the bronze bears his portrait.

While photographing the sculpture in Liverpool, I asked one of the women clerks in Lewis's if she knew the meaning of the sun god over the entrance to the store. She told me, of course, she did, and said that it meant the symbolic rising of the Youth of Liverpool from the ashes of the bombing of the city during the War. She also said that Epstein had come to the city while great sections of it lay in ruins after the German bombings, and he had looked at the landscape. This visiting the site was a practice Epstein always employed whenever possible before designing his sculpture for architecture and natural settings. It is therefore important that photographs of such monumental pieces include the surroundings, whenever possible; otherwise part of the artist's conception is lost.

Echoes of the Wilde Tomb and Whitman's poetry are found in *The Liverpool Giant*. The children represented at play on the bas-reliefs below the great giant are now almost totally blackened by the grime of Liverpool, but it is possible to see the baby, Epstein's grandaughter, Annabel Freud, seated in her carriage, holding out her arms. She carries a minature version of the Epstein face on her features. Her arms are outstretched in the attitude of the goddess and the *Majestas* of Llandaff. The little girl in the carriage is the female counterpart of Man, (and of God), the Queen, who carries Man's soul back to Heaven, according to Kabbalistic writings. Reference here also can be found to the New Testament, Mark 9, 36-38 and Mark 10,13-17, to Jesus's remarks about the entrance to Heaven through little children. The boys and girls, happily playing on either side as the baby watches, echo the ringing cries and joy of the children at play on Hester Street, the concourse of markets and shops for immigrant Jews in New York City. The interior of Lewis's carries on its first floor a complete food market, as do the stores in Israel and other parts of Europe. We are apt to forget that supermarkets are a relatively new idea, developed after World War Two. This store undoubtedly stimulated early memories in Epstein, possibly of his little sister Sylvia and her friends, when he came to see the site selected for his great bronze.

St. Michael and the Devil 1958, New Coventry Cathedral, and *Majestas*, 1955, Llandaff Cathedral, Llandaff, Cardiff, Wales, are two works which are best studied together, although the *Majestas* was first completed and installed under Epstein's direction. *Christ in Majesty*, or *Majestas*, in Llandaff Cathedral is the final conception of the great circle of Life first developed in the lovely little girl, *The Visitation*, 1926, which bears the face of Sylvia Epstein. As Mrs. Press herself has mentioned, her brother wished to do a Madonna and Child of her with Peggy Jean when she visited them in 1928. This probably was later completed by Epstein in the *Madonna of Cavendish Square*, which was originally conceived bearing the features of his second wife, Lady Kathleen. The ancient gothic cathedral was visited by Epstein before his work on the commission began. I was told by Mr. Neville James, a parishioner, that Epstein came to view the church, which had had its roof destroyed by bombings. The walls and nave were left intact. Epstein designed a monumental aluminum Christ-God-Holy Spirit figure to encompass the concrete structure which holds the organ. It is supported on either side by huge concrete arches; the sculpture and the organ seem to float above the heads of the worshippers in the center of the nave. The church is luminous, in fact flooded by light from the old clerestories.

At Evensong the cathedral and *Majestas* are lit by a slow ebbing light. The combination of the formal service of the Church of England, the great pipe organ music, and the compassionate and melancholy *Majestas*, the Divine Wisdom and God, clothed in the white light described by the Kabbalah as God's light – this is Epstein in his greatest development. The Ancient of Ancients, the *Majestas*, has but one face, the faces of Man – here the final version of the Epstein face grown old. The bony protuberance under the eyes is very prominent – Hyman, Sylvia, Mary, Marthe – even Chatskel – and Sunita – they are all there, along with Jacob, whose name also means Israel. This is a masterpiece.

St. Michael and the Devil, although executed later, is the final act of transmigration of the soul, just before the Devil is reabsorbed into God the Father. The monster at Coventry is the snake man; the body is now in process of changing. The torso of St. Michael is a triumphant reworking of the softly beautiful, Italianate *Lucifer* of 1944, but here Michael's body is that of the vigorous young sun god, Roman soldier and statesman. Handel's *Messiah,* in particular the "Halleluiah Chorus", comes to mind in noting the victory; but in *Green Mansions,* on page 85 of the Modern Library edition previously mentioned, there is an almost complete literary description for the composition of the Coventry *St. Michael and the Devil.* The old Indian Nuflo, the grandfather of Rima, the bird goddess, is describing what is wrong with the world and he mentions having seen a St. Michael on a church in South America – a St. Michael driving a spear into a snake man. Michael here has his foot on the winged monster, a snake man in chains. The first version for the Coventry sculpture, represented by a small *maquette,* included wings on the snake man. There are also descriptions of this victory in the Book of Revelations and in Book Twelve of *Paradise Lost.* The literary qualities of this work overwhelm me and I prefer the *Ecce Homo,* 1935, as Epstein's monument in Coventry.

St. Michael and the Devil is not illustrated here because the personnel at Coventry Cathedral did not approve my photographs which portrayed the artistic intensity of the work. I did not consider the tourist photograph of *St. Michael* which they supplied appropriate for this work, since I had seen it printed on everything from dishtowels to ash trays at Coventry.

The Franklin Medal, 1956, was a commission Epstein received to execute a commemorative medal to Sir Winston Churchill. It was presented to Churchill in Epstein's presence. One can imagine Churchill's inner reaction to this medal, done by "that talented monster", Sir Jacob Epstein. The obverse of the medal has a profile of Franklin; he appears slightly senile, and it is a reworked portrait of the unfinished bust of Churchill, 1946. The reverse side bears a wild portrait of *The Sun God,* his hair flying in all directions as it did on the work done in 1910. *The Sun God* is peering through the bar-like rays of the sun, which he holds in his hand. This work has been described as representing Prometheus, who stole the fire from heaven, but this is also Loki, the Norse god of pranks. The secret joke should be apparent for this is Hymie (Chaim-Hyam) Epstein, whose great-great-uncle was said by Mary Epstein to be Hyam Salomon, financier of the American Revolution. Epstein was an American by birth and Churchill's mother was Jennie Jerome, an American whose father developed the Bronx in New York City. Both Epstein and Churchill were famous figures in English art, politics, and writing, and both were knighted. *The Franklin Medal* is a sardonic reference by Epstein to his superiority to the House of Marlborough, which twice gave him such difficulties with his portraits. I think this also contains another hidden gibe by Epstein, and indicates his belief that art, in particular his art, which was based on literary allegory in the great English tradition, and on the Judeo-Christian cultures of two continents, would outlast Churchill's achievements.

In 1954 Epstein completed the commission for the Fairmount Park Art Association in Philadelphia – *Social Consciousness.* The artist says that it is based on Walt Whitman's poem *America* and in his book, *Epstein, an Autobiography,*[10] he gives his interpretation, quoting from two lines he says he has illustrated. Epstein says that the theme of the first two male figures on the right (left of the viewer) is the healer supporting humanity. On the left (right of viewer) the eternal

---

mother supports future humanity and the concept of Time is placed in the center. The two lines which are engraved on the base of the sculpture are as follows:

A grand, sane, towering, seated Mother,
Chair'd in the adamant of Time.

One should note the circular reference of Epstein's words; the seated figure is mentioned last. Although criticism has been levelled at this work's composition, it is unjustified, for the composition is a mental one – a great circle.

One starts on the viewer's left with the two male figures, which represent the family tragedy of the Epsteins; the two figures are interchangeable – Jacob and Hyman, The Sun God. It should be noted that the Christ is faceless here. The eye then travels to the right, to the young Queen of Heaven. She supports the rising Christ, Prince of Light. Christ now has a face. The viewer's gaze ends in the center, on the seated female/male figure of the Great Mother – Genesis, Time, Light. The Great Mother bears the face of Mary Epstein, the Epstein face, the Ancient of Ancients. It is also the face of Jacob, Margaret as represented on the Lazarus, and Sunita – the Orient.

This conception is Epstein's farewell to America; it is also his tomb here. It was executed five years before his death. It seems to say: "All is over, all is forgiven." The synthesis of Whitman's poetry is here, for one must read more than just the poem *America*. Other important poems are *When Lilacs Last in the Doorway Bloom'd, Song of Myself,* and *A Broadway Pageant.* The entire poem America is reprinted here:

Centre of equal daughters, equal sons.
All, all alike endear'd, grown, ungrown, young or old,
Strong, ample, fair, enduring, capable, rich,
Perennial with the Earth, with Freedom, Law and Love,
A grand, sane, towering, seated Mother,
Chair'd in the adamant of Time.

The Kabbalistic books of the Beginning and End, Genesis and Light, have been completed in this work. There are echoes here of the Adams and Bigelow Memorials, particularly in the mystic center figure, but the malevolent sphinx has been overcome. The young male figures of this work contain the same grace I saw on the early 1902 photographs of Epstein's student work in Paris. It is probably impossible to know now whether this was a conscious or unconscious reprise in 1954.

While photographing the work in 1976 I saw a young Israeli family come up to the *Social Consciousness.* I stopped work to watch their reaction to the group. The young father looked at it and then said something in Hebrew to his young wife. She took the little girl (there were three of them) up to the Great Mother, and the little girl climbed up onto the lap of the great bronze figure. The father took her picture. When I later told Mrs. Clamage, Epstein's niece, about this, she remarked: "Uncle Jacob would have liked that."

The *Bowater House Group*, a bronze composition of five allegorical figures, was cast after Epstein's death. The artist completed and approved the clay composition for the plaster mold on the day he died[11]. The great bronzes were placed in Hyde Park, directly in front of Bowater House, headquarters for one of England's largest iron foundries. As Buckle has noted in his book, the work owes a great deal to the Rudé *Marseillaise* on the Arc de Triomphe in Paris. However, there are also other elements in this work which can now be explored. The grouping of the figures recalls the work of Epstein's early teacher, George Grey Barnard. The male figure carries the Epstein face, and his fist is outstretched in the Greek athlete's salute to the crowd. The flowing, druid-like female also bears the Epstein face, but the god Pan, god of sensual love, art and music, carries the realistic portrait of the old Jewish rabbi. One can see that face today at the Wailing Wall in Jerusalem. The child's importance is now obvious, as is the dog's; they are both transcendental figures. The whole group also stretches out its arms in the great Hebrew drinking toast – L'Chaim, To Life.

11 Buckle, op. cit. pp. 414-422.

Richard Buckle also remarks that, seeing Epstein's work at the end of his life, one asks what the fuss was all about? The answer is that it was about quite a lot. When Epstein arrived in Paris in 1902, the great French artist was Auguste Rodin. Rodin explored the sensual aspects of man's relations in a manner directly traceable to the beginnings of the breakdown of Calvinistic precepts. The Puritan idea of the relationship of men and women as brother and sister, mother and father, tending the Garden of Eden, and rising above the abasing sexual desires, was being driven out by the hypocrisy of the lives led in Europe. The premise was false and Sigmund Freud had begun to tell people so, through his break-throughs in psychoanalysis.

Yet Rodin's art, which has also many elements of the then-popular Art Nouveau Movement, veiled these states of mind with blurred and elevated references to Romanticism and Classicism. Art Nouveau posters and magazine illustrations showed the feminine ideal as a buxom young woman with flowing hair in which flowers were entwined. Her diaphanous garments revealed a veiled breast and the complete frontal pelvic region. Audrey Beardsley's art was filled with erotic symbols, all beautifully drawn and hidden as puzzles within the lines of the sketches. How much of this was done under the influence of drugs is not known, but this is a style which resurfaces in our drug culture of the 1960s.

Freud was needed badly, however misinterpreted by later feminists. Women were denying their pregnancies and sexual lives. They dressed in concealing clothes up until the birth of the child, and often wore corsets which deformed and created difficult births. When the child was born, everyone pretended that it had descended from heaven, or had been found under a cabbage leaf. Life in London before the Great War was licentious and full of vice. Edward VII was a notorious womanizer. The young Epstein began to show life as it really was. Women have big bellies when they are pregnant. *The Genesis,* 1930, reveals how women actually feel and look during pregnancy. Some of Epstein's women in portraits are shown with the swollen breasts of pregnancy and nursing. His mythological figures show women in orgasm.

A cartoon from *Punch,* first published on June 3, 1925[12], gives public reaction to Epstein's *Hudson Memorial.* A beautiful, Georgian Eros is shooting an arrow at Epstein's Rima. The caption reads, in full, as follows:

FOR THIS RELIEF NOT MUCH THANKS.

Epstein's female: "KAMERAD!"

Gilbert's Eros: "I THINK NOT."

English taste in art and decoration was then neo-Georgian and conservative. Even Betty Joel's avant-garde designs for English modern furniture are refined and restrained versions of the more daring French experiments of this time. The rough, elemental quality of Epstein's bird goddess, her roots in the Hester Street and Russian-Polish ghettoes of Europe, was very disturbing. Anti-Semitism was growing and it must be remembered that the new Russian Communist State had overthrown, and killed, the Czar, a cousin to George V. Epstein's art was not just a reworking of old ideas, however tame it may now seem.

Although Europe would not face it, Germany was marching the Jews into the concentration camps in the 1930s. The cosmic rage of *Adam,* 1938, does not deal only with Whitman and the fecundity of man. If one can not deal with something which shocks and enrages, one can always try to make it go away by laughing and deriding it. This was what the public did to Epstein. But the thing does not go away. It is still here. This is what the artist was saying.

When I visited the Epstein monumental art works in Europe, I was quite shocked by the condition into which they have fallen. Although his art may now be considered by some to be old-

11 Buckle, *op. cit.,* pp. 414-422.

12 Melly, George and Glaves-Smith, J.R., *A Child of Six Could Do It!,100 Years of Cartoons About Modern Art,* The Tate Gallery/ Barrons, London, 1973, pp. 44-45.

fashioned, this is far from the truth. It is disturbing to see that the penis has been ripped of and broken on the Wilde Tomb. Graffiti has been scratched on the sculpture. Interestingly, it is all in English and appears to be quite recent. Much of it is in defence of homosexuality.

Air pollution is destroying the Rima memorial; the features of the bird girl can hardly be seen. Algae are growing on the marble. The deterioration of the Liverpool bronze and maquettes is obvious from my photographs. Epstein himself first alerted England to this danger when he examined the crumbling statues of his *Four Stages of Life*, and found that a lead water plate was eroding the concrete by dripping directly on it.

The parishioners of Riverside Church have unknowingly altered the original concept of the plaster model for the Majestas, now displayed over a dark balcony. The plaster has been gilded; the artist's ideas have been totally altered. The extraordinary face is not visible. The sculpture should not have been painted nor the lighting rearranged by spots. Epstein himself designed the work to fit the mystic concept and the ancient site at Llandaff Cathedral.

People react to Epstein's art with bafflement, but they sense part of his themes. The concepts tantalize and elude them, and this is as it should be. When I came to Llandaff to photograph the *Majestas*, I was most kindly assisted by Mr. Neville James, who went with me as I climbed on top of the roof and shot pictures through the clerestory windows. Mr. James said to me, in referring to the Christ: "It's the family, isn't it? We've always thought so. He was here, you know. It looks like him."

"It's his father," I said, for at that time I had been pursuing the theme from that angle. When I returned home, I began to consider our reactions to the work. At first I thought I was correct and Mr. James was wrong. Later I saw that he was correct. Now I know that we both are.

80

INDEX